BE STILL
& SOAR

Praise for *Be Still & Soar*

"Nora Plesent is a treasure; a font of wisdom and compassion. In this book she generously shares everything she knows about how to live a more centered and more peaceful life, and you will benefit from it, I promise."

— *Nina Lorez Collins, Chief Creative Officer, Hello Revel, and founder, The Woolfer*

"So often we're too overwhelmed and tired to access resources that can help us hold what is happening. This is a perfect book to reach for when we need a bite-size serving of calm and wisdom. How lovely to have the teachings of the ages curated by Nora and served in manageable pieces."

— *Rabbi Amy Bernstein, Senior Rabbi, Kehillat Israel, Pacific Palisades, CA*

"Nora Plesent writes with the voices of Wisdom, Experience, and Compassion permeating her tonality. From her piercing moments of self-understanding to her characterizations of distilled life experiences through the words of other great writers, thinkers, leaders, and just plain folks, she keeps us turning the pages to be nourished by the next idea and its application.

Never preachy or condescending, she manages to speak to us from one of life's most sacred perches: the summit of a survivor who has walked (and is still walking) the path through life's maze of joys and heartbreaks, its pitfalls and moments of promise. Join her, friends."

— *The Rev. Dr. John Fairless, Gainesville, Florida*

"The book you have in your hands will inspire you to reflect. Nora has woven together personal observations with wise, compelling and soothing quotes. Her words feel as if she is right next to you whispering, "I understand, and we can get through this together."

— *Heather Hayward, Creator of*
The Guided Meditation Framework

Praise for *Be Still & Soar*

"Nora Plesent is a treasure; a font of wisdom and compassion. In this book she generously shares everything she knows about how to live a more centered and more peaceful life, and you will benefit from it, I promise."

— *Nina Lorez Collins, Chief Creative Officer, Hello Revel, and founder, The Woolfer*

"So often we're too overwhelmed and tired to access resources that can help us hold what is happening. This is a perfect book to reach for when we need a bite-size serving of calm and wisdom. How lovely to have the teachings of the ages curated by Nora and served in manageable pieces."

— *Rabbi Amy Bernstein, Senior Rabbi, Kehillat Israel, Pacific Palisades, CA*

"Nora Plesent writes with the voices of Wisdom, Experience, and Compassion permeating her tonality. From her piercing moments of self-understanding to her characterizations of distilled life experiences through the words of other great writers, thinkers, leaders, and just plain folks, she keeps us turning the pages to be nourished by the next idea and its application.

Never preachy or condescending, she manages to speak to us from one of life's most sacred perches: the summit of a survivor who has walked (and is still walking) the path through life's maze of joys and heartbreaks, its pitfalls and moments of promise. Join her, friends."

— *The Rev. Dr. John Fairless, Gainesville, Florida*

"The book you have in your hands will inspire you to reflect. Nora has woven together personal observations with wise, compelling and soothing quotes. Her words feel as if she is right next to you whispering, "I understand, and we can get through this together."

— *Heather Hayward, Creator of*
The Guided Meditation Framework

BE STILL & SOAR

Finding Strength and Solace in Any Storm

Nora Plesent

The Gathering Press
Los Angeles, California

Be Still & Soar

Copyright © 2022 by Nora Plesent

Published by The Gathering Press,
Los Angeles, California

All rights reserved. This book or parts thereof may not be reproduced in any form, stored in any retrieval system, or transmitted in any form by any means—electronic, mechanical, photocopy, recording, or otherwise—without prior written permission of the publisher, except as provided by United States of America copyright law. For information regarding permission requests, write to nora@noraplesent.com.

ISBNs:
979-8-9851759-1-2 hardcover
979-8-9851759-2-9 paperback
979-8-9851759-0-5 ebook
979-8-9851759-3-6 audiobook

Editing and Permissions: Anna Schnur-Fishman
Book design: Carla Green, Clarity Designworks

By reading this document, the reader agrees that under no circumstances is the author or the publisher responsible for any losses, direct or indirect, which are incurred as a result of the use of the information contained within this document, including, but not limited to, errors, omissions, or inaccuracies.

www.noraplesent.com

This book is dedicated to my brother Mark, who inspired us all by living a life of passion, purpose, and presence.

CONTENTS

Introduction xi

1 New Normal.................................1
2 One Day at a Time...........................4
3 Being Present Is Powerful....................7
4 Allow Yourself to Wander 10
5 The Honeymoon Is Over......................12
6 Take Care of Your Inner Being 15
7 The Fog Will Move On 18
8 Take Back Control..........................20
9 Become Familiar to Yourself 23
10 Wisdom Extracted..........................26
11 Moments of Being 29
12 Earth Is Forgiveness School 32
13 The Ripple Effect 36
14 Uncertainty Is Certain 40
15 Embracing Vulnerabilities 44
16 Worrier or Warrior 48
17 Patience Is a Gift 52
18 Connection Is the Antidote to Fear............55
19 See Beneath Your Beautiful 60

20	RBG as a Spiritual Leader	64
21	Window or Aisle Seat	69
22	This Too...	74
23	Love Is the Answer	79
24	Take Your Broken Heart and Turn it into Art	84
25	I'm Shrinking	90
26	When Will This Be Over?	96
27	Why Don't We Feel Elated?	102
28	Shake It Off	108
29	Thank the Givers	113
30	What You Don't Appreciate, Depreciates	116
31	What Is Humble Pie?	120
32	Our Need For Belonging	126
33	Open the Doors Within Us	132
34	The Weight of Waiting	136
35	Is Self-Compassion Selfish?	141
36	The Importance of a "Trust Fund"	148
37	To Everything there Is a Season	154
38	A Room of One's Own	161
39	Thriving Rather Than Striving	168
40	A Flood of Tears	177
41	Radical Love	187
42	Let the Love In	195
43	Are We Ready to Spring Forward?	204

Credits	209
About the Author	213

INTRODUCTION

Where do you go when the world seems dark and scary? To whom do you turn when life is upside down?

How do you keep going when things around you are falling apart? Where do you find strength when fear and loss are tearing at your heart? How do you make sense out of unexpected changes?

These are the questions that prompted this book, *Be Still & Soar.*

When COVID-19 hit, we found ourselves locked down: unable to be with those we love, uncertain of what each day would bring, afraid for our lives. The following months wreaked havoc on our nervous systems. Anxiety, depression, fear and overwhelm rooted in our bodies and minds.

Unable to conduct mindfulness coaching and retreats in person, I began writing a newsletter to my clients. It was as much for myself as for others. As I dug deep each week to figure out how I was doing, to identify glimpses of hope, to manifest bits of calm in the chaos, I would share my findings.

And I was reminded that it was not the first time I tumbled, head over heels, into a scary and destabilizing unknown.

I had left a 17-year marriage.

I had walked away from a law firm partnership to build my own company from scratch.

I had moved across the country as a single parent of four.

I had lost a brother, much too young, on the very same day I first held my fourth child. (And I was to lose my second brother, fourteen years later but still much too early, within the first year of the pandemic.)

My clients responded deeply to that weekly newsletter, and as a result, I realized what I knew about resilience in the face of loss, pain, fear, isolation, disappointment and uncertainty. They were universal challenges and universal truths. Mindfulness, an incredible gift, supported my growth at every turn, no matter the situation.

By opening ourselves up, slowing down, being vulnerable, reflective and honest, we can alter how our lives look and feel. We can deepen our understanding of ourselves, our surroundings, and our world by asking poignant questions and listening to our own voices from within.

It is my honor to share my thoughts and reflections with you for those moments when you need a new perspective, a bit of hope, or a dose of wisdom.

1
NEW NORMAL

Dear All,

This is a time of tremendous uncertainty and it's very normal to have difficulty focusing.

We are in unchartered waters and doing our best to acclimate to a life within the home, with almost no in-person connection with others. Many of you are finding interesting new ways to spend time, while others may be overwhelmed with the burden of family and work responsibilities with very little time to yourself.

In a single day there may be joy, frustration, anger, appreciation, and impatience. Whatever you are feeling, allow that. What is important during these times is to acknowledge what's going on for you and to be compassionate to yourself and to others. We all need to be given a break!

Now, more than ever, it is helpful to take time to go inside yourself and connect with your still, small voice.

It is important to take time to nourish your soul and not get caught up in the frenzy of social media, news, podcasts, and anything else that takes away from your inner contemplation.

"Quiet the mind and the soul will speak."
— *Ma Jaya Sati Bhagavati*

My commitment is to nurture you all. I am sending you all lots of hugs and love and support.

With love and light,
Nora

Quiet the mind
and the soul
will speak.

Ma Jaya Sati Bhagavati

2
ONE DAY AT A TIME

Dear All,

I hope you are all managing through this strange and scary time.

While you may have had some wonderful moments of slowing down, reconnecting with an old friend, or baking something special, you may also be feeling anxious, moody, unable to sleep, and be experiencing sadness, uncertainty, and grief. Try to allow yourself to feel whatever you are feeling, day to day, moment to moment.

> "One of the loneliest elements of exile is the exile from one's feelings. The person who is not able to feel his life has become dangerously dislocated. Sometimes severe suffering causes this numbing: the heart atrophies." — *John O'Donohue*

Connect with your own feelings and make sure your heart doesn't atrophy. I am committed to helping you become calmer and clearer so that your heart opens wide and inspired action follows.

It is important to take time to nourish your soul with poetry, music, and the company of wise and wonderful women. Make time for you.

> With love and light,
> *Nora*

One of the loneliest elements of exile is the exile from one's feelings. The person who is not able to feel his life has become dangerously dislocated. Sometimes severe suffering causes this numbing: the heart atrophies.

John O'Donohue

3

BEING PRESENT IS POWERFUL

Dear All,

What is your biggest challenge this week?

» Some of us are wishing we had our old lives back.
» Some of us don't want to go back to the lives we had.
» Some of us are grieving—others, worried about finances.
» Some of us wish we could see people we are missing.
» Some of us are wishing we could get away from the people around us.
» Some of us are bored and others are exhausted.

No matter where you are, it's where you need to be. Be open to the lessons you need to learn and embrace them. Practice being in the present.

"If you separate from . . . everything you have done in the past, everything that disturbs you about the future . . . and apply yourself to living the life that you are living that is to say, the present, you can live all the time that remains to you . . . in calm, benevolence and serenity." — *Marcus Aurelius*

It's a time when we may need more support than we even know.

Surround yourself with people who will inspire you, read books that speak to your soul, be out in nature as much as possible, and try to meditate.

Allow yourself to be supported on your journey to contentment, peace, and joy.

With love and light,
Nora

If you separate from . . .
Everything you have done
in the past, everything
that disturbs you about
the future . . . And apply
yourself to living the
life that you are living
that is to say, the
present, you can live all
the time that remains to
you . . . In calm, benevolence
and serenity.

Marcus Aurelius

4

ALLOW YOURSELF TO WANDER

Dear All,

You made it through another week! The days feel long, but the weeks go by quickly! Things are changing, yet remaining the same. One minute you may be enjoying a special moment on Facetime with an old friend and the next moment you may burst out in tears for no particular reason. This is the time to be tolerant of others and particularly yourself. We are all winging it so perfection doesn't exist (actually, it never did!). We are all on this bumpy road together. Allow yourself to wander, meander, be open to what's in front of you, and be surprised.

In the words of Theodore Roethke: "I learn by going where I have to go."

And for most of us right now, we are on new paths, finding where it is we have to go.

With love and light,
Nora

I learn by going where I have to go.

Theodore Roethke

5
THE HONEYMOON IS OVER

Dear All,

You may be feeling down, edgy, bored, worried or exhausted. The "honeymoon" phase of the pandemic is long over and yet, we don't have certainty as to when life will begin to feel less constricted. There is no way around this quarantined existence. We can only go through it, experiencing a whole range of emotions, thoughts, and feelings.

If you have not read Pema Chodron's, When Things Fall Apart, now is the time to devour it. As she says: "Things falling apart is a kind of testing and a kind of healing. We think the point is to pass the test or to overcome the problem, but the truth is that things don't really get solved. They come together and they fall apart again. It's just like that. The healing comes from letting there be room for all of this to happen: room for grief, for relief, for misery, for joy."

Allow for all of it—the exhausting, the depressing, the overwhelming, the tender, the poignancy, the fear.

Taking time to go inside and connect with your inner guidance is not a luxury.

It is what we need.

With love and light,
Nora

Things falling apart is a kind of testing and a kind of healing. We think the point is to pass the test or to overcome the problem, but the truth is that things don't really get solved. They come together and they fall apart again. It's just like that. The healing comes from letting there be room for all of this to happen: room for grief, for relief, for misery, for joy.

Pema Chodron

6
TAKE CARE OF YOUR INNER BEING

Dear All,

We have been in quarantine for three months—a quarter of a year.

Time has slowed down, but emotions are moving through us at rapid speeds. In a single day, we can feel anger, frustration, gratitude, irritation, and despair. We are afraid. We are enraged. We are exhausted. We are cautiously optimistic. We are dealing with what life is throwing at us. We can't take anything else.

There are no answers right now. We are worried about our parents, our kids, our finances, our world. I am right there with you.

I saw Anderson Cooper cry when talking to Professor Cornel West about the humanity exhibited at the funeral of George Floyd. Professor West assured him that tears are an indication of how much we care and that we are not dead inside. I started to cry and, for the first time in a while, hope entered my being. Love really is the answer.

In Cornel West's words: "That's why love is so inseparable from any talk about truth or death, because we know that love is fundamentally a death of an old self that was isolated and the emergence of a new self entangled with another self, the self that you fall in love with."

I believe in the power of love and of self exploration and growth. We can shed our old selves and allow our newer selves to emerge, more loving, more tolerant, more compassionate of others and ourselves.

As Martin Luther King Jr said: "Darkness cannot drive out darkness: only light can do that. Hate cannot drive out hate; only love can do that."

Let's all do our part and love more and more.

Let's start with ourselves.

With love and light,
Nora

That's why love is so inseparable from any talk about truth or death, because we know that love is fundamentally a death of an old self that was isolated and the emergence of a new self entangled with another self, the self that you fall in love with.

Cornel West

7
THE FOG WILL MOVE ON

Dear All,

For many of us, it feels like we are in a thick fog of uncertainty, trying to get through this experience and figure out what's next.

What will we learn from this time?

I am reminded of the iconic poem "Fog" by Carl Sandburg.

> The fog comes
> on little cat feet.
>
> It sits looking
> over harbor and city
> on silent haunches
> and then moves on.

The fog will move on. Who will we be when we re-emerge? Will we miss the comfort of the fog? Will we have greater understanding of the need to sit quietly? Will we have a new vision for the next step in our lives? How will we continue to grow?

With love and light,
Nora

The fog comes
on little cat feet.

It sits looking
over harbor and city
on silent haunches
and then moves on.

Carl Sandburg

8
TAKE BACK CONTROL

Dear All,

Many of us are feeling out of control right now, unable to plan for the immediate future, not knowing whether we will be returning to our old routines or continuing in the more isolated environments of the past few months.

It feels like we are the leaves being blown about rather than the wind itself. There are things to do to feel more in control.

Jack Canfield reminds us that we "only have control over three things in life: the thoughts we think, the images we visualize, and the actions we take."

Meditate each morning by breathing in and out through the nose for at least five minutes. Notice how relaxed you begin to feel almost immediately.

Call a friend and share the feeling of being out of control/scared/anxious. This is a time when we need our friends more than ever. By sharing these feelings, their power over you will subside. You will also be giving someone else the freedom to share their worries and fear.

Get into nature. Nothing brings you closer to yourself than being in the outdoors. The lessons are all around you. You are part of something larger than your challenges of the moment.

Move. The mind can wreak havoc. Let your body take over. Walk, run, dance, bike, surf, whatever! You will feel calmer and more reinvigorated before you know it.

With love and light,
Nora

We only have control over three things in life: the thoughts we think, the images we visualize, and the actions we take.

Jack Canfield

9
BECOME FAMILIAR TO YOURSELF

Dear All,

This week my mother turned ninety-two years old. Although I haven't been able to see her since January, she is always with me.

As we continue to navigate through these uncertain times, I have found that focusing on my core values is really helpful.

There are so many things out of our control right now that it feels like we are swimming against the tide.

My mom has lived her life—through the Great Depression, WWII, and a number of personal tragedies—focused on what she believes is most important. Her core values are optimism, introspection, and patience. I share many of her values and have others of my own, but it has been watching her live according to her values—no matter what—that has taught me so much.

So right now, take a look for yourself at what your top three values are and each day, ask yourself what action you took that reflects each value.

It is a way to help us stay grounded with our truest selves, particularly when things feel so unfamiliar.

Become familiar with yourself by continuing to follow the core values that have made you who you are.

For me, I most value growth, authenticity, and love. The Gathering is a reflection of those values, and I am honored to provide classes for individuals, groups, and companies that are rooted in those values.

In the words of Mahatma Gandhi: "Your beliefs become your thoughts. Your thoughts become your words. Your words become your habits. Your habits become your values. Your values become your destiny."

Values can change. Take some time to reflect on the values that you want to live by. If you want to embrace a new value, do so. Whatever your core values are, believe in them, speak them, act them, and live them.

With love and light,
Nora

Your beliefs become your thoughts.
Your thoughts become your words.
Your words become your habits.
Your habits become your values.
Your values become your destiny.

Mahatma Gandhi

10
WISDOM EXTRACTED

Dear All,

Summer is here but sleepaway camp, outdoor festivals, family barbecues, and travel are not.

For many of us, sheltering in place is getting harder.

Since we cannot change what's happening, all we can work on is how we respond to what's happening.

Last week was a tough one for me. I found myself in a dentist's office having emergency surgery on the same day I was scheduled to move out of my office.

The metaphor was not lost on me. A wisdom tooth extraction!

How would I extract any wisdom in this painful moment?

With a throbbing mouth, I went to pack up the office I have been in for ten years. Not having an office for the first time in forty years will be a huge change! Much of my identity is wrapped up with being a working woman. I was a lawyer for twenty years and a business woman for the next twenty years. Much of my work has been helping women balance families and careers. During those years, I had four kids and after each maternity leave, I returned to my office. I am comfortable in my office, and feel strong and empowered.

But I am being called upon to adapt to a new life. I want to cling to the old, familiar structure, but as Joseph Campbell said, "We must be willing to let go of the life we planned to have the life that is waiting for us."

This is your time. Women spend so much of their lives devoted to helping others in their families, communities, and jobs that they often forget to take care of themselves.

Maya Angelou's quote is perfect for this moment in my life: "The desire to reach for the stars is ambitious. The desire to reach hearts is wise."

As I evolve, I am leaning into the wisdom that comes with the desire to make my life about connecting with others and offering them tools to connect more deeply with themselves.

Let's allow ourselves a little inner peace.

With love and light,
Nora

We must be willing
to let go of the
life we planned to
have the life that is
waiting for us.

Joseph Campbell

11
MOMENTS OF BEING

Dear All,

It was a week of highs and lows. The weather in Los Angeles was exquisite, New York experienced a day without any COVID-19 deaths, my son and his girlfriend arrived for a visit, and California locked down once again due to the rise in infections.

One day I was enjoying an exquisite sunset on the beach while my son and daughter frolicked together in the ocean, and the next day I was crying at my desk as I read an email announcing that schools here would not be open in the fall.

A moment of joy.

A moment of despair.

As Virginia Woolf says, "Life is a series of 'moments of being'." Some exhilarating, some devastating. Moments that make up a life. It is important to remember that it is not the circumstances themselves that dictate the quality of our lives, but rather our response to those circumstances.

Meditation is a meaningful tool to learn to go inside, get quiet, and become comfortable with whatever is happening in the moment. We want to learn to slow down, breathe, feel our feelings (knowing that's all they are), and choose how we want to respond to the events around us. We want to embrace the challenges because they are always moments for growth. And we want to be present to all the wonders and delights happening around us every day. One of my favorite poets, Mary Oliver, writes (in a poem entitled "Moments") that certain moments of being "cry out to be fulfilled"; they call on us to enter them "headlong."

So, to all of you—go headlong into your life. Immerse yourself in everything and you will become more fully alive.

With love and light,
Nora

Life is a series of 'moments of being.'

Virginia Woolf

12
EARTH IS FORGIVENESS SCHOOL

Dear All,

How is everyone doing? I mean really doing.

I spoke to my ninety-two-year-old mother today who said she is in the worst "funk" of her life and she can't find her way out of it.

My mom is one of the most optimistic people I know, so hearing that was a real punch in the gut. I want to fix it, to make easier for her, but I am three thousand miles away and we are in the pandemic. We talked for a long time and, at the end of the call, she said "talking with you lifted my funk." My eyes welled with tears. I felt the healing power of connection.

Other than family, I have had no social interaction for months. But the calls I've had with old and current friends helped lift me out of my own funk on many occasions. However we can, we need to create opportunities to stay connected, particularly when we can't be together physically!

EARTH IS FORGIVENESS SCHOOL

And what about the people we are with physically 24/7? The close quarters in which we are living can put a strain on our closest relationships. No matter how much we love our family members, they can still drive us crazy.

So, this week I've thought a lot about tolerance and forgiveness. Are there people you haven't forgiven for things they did in the past? How many years have you held on to that resentment?

Could you be more tolerant of the people around you?

I love Anne Lamott's honest comment: "I really believe the earth is forgiveness school—I really believe that's why they brought us here, and then left us without any owner's manual."

Forgiveness is hard and ongoing.

My teacher this week was John Lewis, whose words and actions inspired so many people for so many years. The video of him dancing to Pharell Williams's "Happy" filled me with joy. But it is this quote which I have read every day this week and continue to be moved by:

> Anchor the eternity of love in your own soul and embed this planet with goodness. Lean toward the whispers of your own heart, discover the universal truth and follow its dictates. Release the need to hate, to harbor division, and the enticement of revenge. Release all bitterness. Hold only love, only

peace in your heart, knowing that the battle of good to overcome evil is already won.

So inspirational! So aligned with my core values. With meditation, we really can lean toward the whispers of our own heart.

Maya Angelou is quoted as saying, "One of the greatest gifts you can give yourself is to forgive."

Let's work together to create a world with more love, peace, and forgiveness.

And we always have to start with ourselves.

With love and light,
Nora

Anchor the eternity of love in
your own soul and embed this
planet with goodness. Lean toward
the whispers of your
own heart, discover the universal
truth and follow its dictates.
Release the need to hate,
to harbor division, and the
enticement of revenge. Release all
bitterness. Hold only
love, only peace in your heart,
knowing that the battle of good
to overcome evil is already won.

John Lewis

13
THE RIPPLE EFFECT

Dear All,

Is it really August?

It's been five months and we still have no idea how long this pandemic will go on.

The fact that the kids are not going back to school is hard to stomach for many of us.

We worry about their intellectual and social growth, their isolation, and boredom.

As adults, we are experiencing many of the same emotions but, in an effort to be strong, we tend not to share our struggles, and instead plow ahead, focusing on what we are grateful for and hoping against hope that our lives will return to normal at some point.

The problem is that we really are in the midst of one of the hardest times in our lives.

We are scared, tired, uncertain, bored, floating in a boat without an oar.

Of course, there are lessons to learn, stories we will share when this is over, but right now, it's hard.

Let yourself experience that. Grieve. Cry. Rage.

THE RIPPLE EFFECT

Feelings need to be felt and luckily, they do dissipate. You can always take a moment, get quiet and connect with the peaceful, knowing, and loving place inside of you, which, thankfully, is always available to us.

For me, I need to listen to voices that are both authentic and inspiring. I heard Michelle Obama's inaugural episode of her podcast where she interviewed her husband. I couldn't stop smiling as I listened to the two of them—their banter, jokes, love, and commonality so evident. They talked a lot about the importance of community, having something bigger than either one of them individually.

Most of us are aching for community right now, and it's up to us to create whatever we can to give us that feeling of being part of something, being included, known, belonging.

Maybe it's our family right now, or a few friends. It may feel small, but perhaps it's more powerful.

Whatever community means to us, this is a time to embrace what, or who, makes us feel safe and loved.

The beauty of real community is that we are naturally drawn to give to others what we want and need.

The world is hurting right now and how we can make a real difference in our communities feels daunting.

I heed the words Mother Teresa is quoted as saying: "I alone cannot change the world, but I can cast a stone across the waters to create many ripples." So, cast your stones of love, presence, generosity, and understanding, and see how they ripple out.

The wonderful poet and philosopher Yung Pueblo concurs: "Humans affect one another deeply, in ways that the world at large is just beginning to understand. . . . When we heal ourselves it gives strength to those who need more support to take on their own personal healing journey. What we do reverberates through time and space—like a rock thrown into a lake, the circles it creates move in all directions."

So, keep being good to yourselves—be patient and compassionate, and let up on the judgments and self-criticism.

My commitment is to nurture you in ways you don't nurture yourself. That is the rock I am throwing into the lake, sending ripples of love and support out to all of you, particularly all the women who give, give, give, and give to everyone else. I know how exhausting it is.

With love and light,
Nora

I alone cannot change
the world, but I can
cast a stone across
the waters to create
many ripples.

Mother Teresa

14
UNCERTAINTY IS CERTAIN

Dear All,

Uncertainty may be the word of 2020, but hearing and reading it over and over does not make living with it any easier.

The truth is that uncertainty makes us tense up, physically and emotionally, and we start trying to control anything and everything we can. Unfortunately, that urge to control keeps us stuck in a repetitive cycle of worry-control-disappointment-frustration, without any space to breathe, think clearly, or consider events from a new perspective.

Although we've always had uncertainty in our lives, this time feels different and our worrying about our health, our children, our parents, our jobs, our finances, our country, and the world seems universal.

So, how do we manage this uncertainty and worry?

We need to lean into the uncertainty and begin to recognize the sensations, thoughts, and feelings we are experiencing. As we invite those feelings in, the uncertainty begins to loosen its hold on us, and we can HAVE the feeling rather than BE the feeling.

Staying open is key. Suzuki Roshi, a Buddist master, talks about the importance of allowing in the uncertainty and not looking for answers or solutions. His famous quote, "In the beginner's mind there are many possibilities but in the expert's mind there are few," is particularly instructive in these times.

As we learn to cultivate the "beginner's mind," we can feel the body relaxing, our mind opening, and our capacity for wonder expanding.

Margaret Drabble, one of my favorite authors, writes, "When nothing is sure, anything is possible."

For me, the uncertainty of not knowing when I will see my aging parents, my brother who is ill or my kids on the east coast, feels like I am being strangled. I try to meditate more, walk more, write more, and express my love more. And I try to stay with the feelings associated with the worry and uncertainty.

Ultimately, it's all about letting go, and we are encouraged to repeat those words, "let go" as often and regularly as we can. Breathing in, "letting," and breathing out, "go." Repeat.

Your rigidity will become softness, your tension will melt into relaxation, and your certainty will become openness.

In the words of e.e. cummings, "let all go / dear / so comes love."

Stay open, come from a beginner's mind, allow all possibilities, and let go.

So comes love.

With love and light,
Nora

When nothing is sure,
anything is possible.

Margaret Drabble

15

EMBRACING VULNERABILITIES

Dear All,

The word "vulnerability" makes many of us cringe—particularly those of us for whom outward success has played an important role. We do everything in our power to keep our vulnerabilities hidden so that we can be seen as strong and unstoppable. We want the world to know that we are capable of moving through life powerfully. But of course, we all have vulnerabilities and hiding them is oddly counterproductive. They become frightening to us only when we label them as weak, unwanted parts of ourselves. The truth is that embracing them makes us stronger and more authentic.

Brené Brown says: "Vulnerability is the birthplace of love, belonging, joy, courage, empathy, and creativity. It is the source of hope, empathy, accountability, and authenticity. If we want greater clarity in our purpose or deeper and more meaningful spiritual lives, vulnerability is the path."

EMBRACING VULNERABILITIES

When I think about the people I have been drawn to throughout my life, I recognize that they have all been comfortable with their vulnerability. Truthfully, it's often people's vulnerabilities that attract us to them.

The writer and feminist, Audre Lorde, agrees and writes, "That visibility which makes us most vulnerable is that which also is the source of our greatest strength."

I am feeling more vulnerable than usual these days, worried that I am not doing enough for my parents and my kids during these trying times. I am irritated with myself for not being more productive, organized, focused. I continually need to be more tolerant and patient. There are times when I feel I am paddling upstream without a paddle. I have shed a lot of tears this week—for my family and our country—and have felt helpless to make a real difference. It's not easy to express these sides of ourselves, but it is human.

I know that these qualities of vulnerability only make me more deeply connected to myself and that the more I invite them in, the "deeper and more spiritual" a life I will have.

I hope you will consider giving yourself a break, letting your vulnerabilities snuggle up right next to all your strengths, joining forces so that you can feel more at peace with, and accepting of who, you truly are. I honor your courage to do so.

In the words of Madeleine L'Engle, "When we were children, we used to think that when we were grown up we would no longer be vulnerable. But to grow up is to accept vulnerability."

To be alive is to be vulnerable.

With love and light,
Nora

When we were children, we used to think that when we were grown up we would no longer be vulnerable. But to grow up is to accept vulnerability.

Madeleine L'Engle

16
WORRIER OR WARRIOR

Dear All,

Are you a worrier or a warrior?

I have been a worrier my entire life. When I first heard the word "catastrophizing," I felt understood! That's exactly what I would do—imagine the worst possible outcome of a situation and convince myself of its probability.

I am not alone. Worrying is universal; in fact, our nervous systems are set up to worry.

So how do we manage this debilitating habit?

My meditation practice has been hugely helpful, and I can say that I am less of a worrier and more of a warrior than ever before.

But worrying doesn't just go away. It kind of nestles its way into our brain on a pretty regular basis. Noticing when we begin to worry is very helpful. Pay attention to the moment a worry thought comes into your head. Then notice what emotion follows. Finally, see what is happening to the body when you have worrisome thoughts and feelings.

Sit down, close your eyes and take several long deep breaths, repeating "everything is alright" on the inhalation and "right now" on the exhalation. Repeat several times and see if your body relaxes, shaking off the tension and allowing you to breathe in more rational thinking.

Because most likely, everything actually is alright right now.

As Janis Joplin, one of my favorite singers, said, "You can destroy your now by worrying about tomorrow."

Worrying will never change the result so it's definitely worth doing what we can to unhook ourselves from the addictive habit of worrying. There are several things to try:

- » Ask yourself, "What do I believe?"
- » Then ask yourself, "Is what I believe about this situation true?"
- » Consider whether there is a less negative way to think about the situation.
- » Ask yourself, "What would I tell a friend with this worry?"
- » Get up and move!
- » Take a few conscious breaths.
- » Meditate

Here's what Winston Churchill has to say about worrying: "Everyone remembers the remark of the old man at the point of death: that his life had been full of troubles, most of which had never happened."

Such a poignant message!

May we all heed the wisdom of this Chinese proverb: "That the birds of worry and care fly over your head, this you cannot change. But that they build a nest in your hair, this you can prevent."

Here's to all of you!

With love and light,
Nora

That the birds of worry
and care fly over your
head, this you cannot
change. But that they
build a nest in your hair,
this you can prevent.

Chinese proverb

17
PATIENCE IS A GIFT

Dear All,

My father has always been my moral compass. His words always align with his actions, making them even more impactful. He is a man of true integrity.

When I would share a challenge I was experiencing, personally or professionally, his response was usually just a few words, "Patience and Fortitude."

I had a hard time with patience. I didn't fully understand its importance and, in fact, thought there was something passive about it. When I was striving to succeed in my career, I thought that being impatient was a healthy tool to keep going. Later, when I was a single working mom of four, I didn't understand how I could ever find the time to become patient.

It has taken me over fifty years to really heed the wisdom my dad's words.

In Judith Orloff's book, *Emotional Freedom*, she talks about how we can deal with all sorts of frustrations by practicing patience. She describes the energy of frustration as tense, prickly, trapped in your head, and frayed at the edges. Conversely, the energy of patience feels generous, appreciative, respectful—like a big exhale. It has been my journey to becoming an immersive meditation leader that has finally connected me to the gift of patience both as a way to combat frustration, but also as a way to stop getting in my own way.

My dad has never meditated nor read a book about emotional freedom, but instinctively knew the power of patience and fortitude. I am grateful that he has been patient with me as I have learned his lessons in my own way and my own time.

I want to be more generous, appreciative, respectful, and less tense, prickly, and frayed at the edges.

I also finally understand that there's no rush.

"Nature does not hurry, yet everything is accomplished." — *Lao Tse*

Imagine there's enough time to find your way, your purpose, your person, your calm. Because when we cultivate patience and experience—its calming, soft, embracing presence—there really is time to do what we need and want to do to be fully self-expressed. When we eliminate the barriers to our most authentic nature, we can experience the flow of our lives. We can experience that big exhale we all yearn for.

With love and light,
Nora

Nature does not hurry,
yet everything is accomplished.

Lao Tse

18

CONNECTION IS THE ANTIDOTE TO FEAR

Dear All,

There's a lot to be afraid about these days—the economy, politics, COVID-19, isolation, and wildfires for starters!

And we all have our own personal challenges as well!

This week, I had a situation with a family member that was terrifying for me.

Unfortunately, we have been taught to avoid fear, fear fear, and try to live life without fear.

The truth is that we will always have fear—our nervous systems are wired so that we are prepared for attacks by predators!

As Eleanor Roosevelt wrote, "You gain strength, courage, and confidence by every experience in which you really stop to look fear in the face. . . . You must do the thing you think you cannot do."

So how do we handle fear and even learn the secret of life from it?

It's helpful to notice when we first experience it and to accurately assess the current fear-inducing situation.

We can start by asking ourselves, "What do you believe is happening that may not be true?"

We can also check in with our body sensations and see where we are holding on, where there's strain or tightness and breathe into that area, softening and letting go.

It's helpful to bring to mind an image that is particularly calming, and just focus on and breathe in that image for several breaths.

We can also choose a few empowering words, something like, "I have fear, but my fear does not have me," and breathe in and out several times, repeating the words to yourself.

Touch is also a proven way to minimize fear so try hugging a loved one or a pet or even squeezing your own hand, providing a comforting sensation.

Finally, connection is the antidote to fear.

The words of Rumi in "Search the Darkness," as translated by Kabir Helminksi, are particularly helpful:

Sit with your friends; don't go back to sleep.
Don't sink like a fish to the bottom of the sea.

Surge like an ocean,
don't scatter yourself like a storm.

CONNECTION IS THE ANTIDOTE TO FEAR

Life's waters flow from darkness.
Search the darkness, don't run from it.

Night travelers are full of light,
and you are, too; don't leave this companionship.

Be a wakeful candle in a golden dish,
don't slip in the dirt like quicksilver.

The moon appears for night travelers,
be watchful when the moon is full.

I often feel like separating myself from others when I am in fear. I am uncertain of how to express my fear without embarrassment and often choose to "grin and bear it."

Instead, I need to remember the words of Rumi, that we are all living in fear but connected with each other. It is important that we not "leave this companionship," that we acknowledge that we are not alone.

There are benefits to surrounding yourselves with people who are positive, authentic, and open, willing to "search the darkness" with you, and not run from it.

Acknowledge your fear and move through the fearful emotions, thoughts, and bodily sensations. Allow your fear to sit next to you, reminding you that you have fear but that you are not your fear.

BE STILL & SOAR

Finish the statement: "With my fear beside me, I can now . . ."

Listen and be guided.

You are strong, safe, and supported.

Remember that we are all in this together.

With love and light,
Nora

You gain strength, courage, and confidence by every experience in which you really stop to look fear in the face. . . . You must do the thing you think you cannot do.

Eleanor Roosevelt

19

SEE BENEATH YOUR BEAUTIFUL

Dear All,

Many of us have spent our entire lives chasing perfection, being self-critical, frustrated or defeatist when we haven't achieved it.

We often live with a gnawing ache, doing everything to become better, smarter, thinner, nicer, more successful or even more enlightened, just to get closer to that gold ring of perfection.

If we make a wrong choice in our career or relationship, we beat ourselves up.

I am right there with you!

What if instead we could, as Elizabeth Gilbert suggests, "Embrace the glorious mess that [we] are"? Even just saying the phrase to yourself—"I embrace the glorious mess that I am"—may give you a little relief. It feels so good!

We are all imperfect, even those people on Instagram who look perfect!

Our flaws are part of who we are and we would be well-served to embrace them.

The Japanese have a tradition called "kintsugi" (the art of precious scars) which is a process of repairing broken ceramics with gold, leaving a gold seam where the cracks are. By repairing broken objects, it is possible to give them new life—becoming even more refined, not in spite of, but because of, the scars. Rather than hiding/disguising the fractures/flaws, they are celebrated.

Each piece of pottery is presented with its own story and beauty thanks to the cracks.

I was almost in tears reading about this wise and life-affirming practice.

What if we treated our own flaws as integral to who we are?

What if we knew that our cracks were not our destruction but merely part of our history?

What if we could admire our own imperfections?

As Alice Walker says, "Everything is already perfect. And if you can accept that everything is already perfect, the imperfection is part of the perfection. What's to worry about?"

Of course, it's easier said than done, but you can begin by recognizing when there is a negative thought about yourself, slowing down the breath, dropping your shoulders, breathing in "I am imperfect," and breathing out "which makes me perfect."

Do this a few times and see if it helps.

Imagine yourself as a gorgeous piece of pottery, proudly displaying scars with seams of gold for all to see. Take a close look and acknowledge that the scars really do give the piece its uniqueness, its character, and even its charm. You are unique and even more beautiful because of your flaws!

In the iconic words of Leonard Cohen:

There is a crack, a crack in everything.
That's how the light gets in.

Let the light in—let us see beneath your beautiful, embrace the glorious mess that you are.

With love and light,
Nora

Everything is already perfect. And if you can accept that everything is already perfect, the imperfection is part of the perfection. What's to worry about?

Alice Walker

20
RBG AS A SPIRITUAL LEADER

Dear All,

Those of us who remember, know exactly where we were when we learned of President Kennedy's assassination. Many more of us know exactly where we were when our country was attacked on 9/11.

On Friday evening, September 18, 2020, we learned of the death of the incomparable Ruth Bader Ginsburg. That moment will become a defining moment in our lives and in our history. We will never forget where we were when we heard the news.

Many of us were about to attend Rosh Hashana services on Zoom when we got the text/email/alerts. My hero, RBG, was dead. Jewish tradition proclaims that someone who dies on Erev Rosh Hashana is a tzaddik, a righteous being. And she was.

As a young female attorney with children, I revered RBG for the way she unapologetically practiced law and mothered her children. I was awed by her intellect and her wit. I wanted to be her.

Her death so profoundly affected us that we wanted to curl up, get into bed, and never come out. How could we endure another blow? How could we continue to muster hope?

The only way to embrace RBG's teachings is to be steady, patient, trusting, and unwavering in our beliefs. This is our chance to be her.

Rumi says, as translated by Coleman Barks:

> Forget safety. Live where you fear to live.
> Destroy your reputation. Be notorious.

Is that where Notorious RBG came from?

I wouldn't be surprised.

With all that has been written about her this week, I wondered whether there was anything new or important I could add. As I thought about the movies about her, her opinions, her quotes, and the words of so many others who knew her, I realized that RBG was, for me, not only a role model in my legal career, but a spiritual guide. Three of the most important tenets of a spiritual life are:

1. Responding Rather Than Reacting to Life
   RBG often mentioned the advice she received from her mother-in-law, that "in a marriage, it's wise to be a little deaf." She talked about how she believed that to be true for all relationships, including with those on the Supreme Court. "Being a little deaf"

is a thoughtful way to take a pause and respond rather than react to every event or comment thrown at you. It's a way of breathing, something we all need to do more of.

2. Being Compassionate to Ourselves and Others
    We all know what a truly compassionate person RBG was, but she also showed a great deal of self-compassion, a trait fewer of us have. She accepted help, particularly from her husband, who took over the vast majority of household and parenting duties. She embraced, rather than balked at, support and help. In the area of self-compassion, she taught me a lot.

3. Letting Go
    Nothing is more important in living a spiritual life than being able to "let go." Most of us spend our lives holding on to slights, refusing to forgive ourselves or others, and clinging to anger and resentment. Ruth Bader Ginsburg had an unusual friendship with Justice Scalia as they shared a great love of opera and food. RBG talked lovingly about her friend, quoting his favorite line: "Get over it." She agreed with him that life is too short to hold on to things and believed in the practice of "letting go" and moving on.

RBG AS A SPIRITUAL LEADER

I don't know whether she considered herself a spiritual person, but RBG's spirit was a gift to us all.

Thank you, RBG, for doing so much for people—particularly women—for believing in our strengths, our lives, and our futures. You will be sorely missed.

These words of the poet Yung Pueblo have given me a great deal of solace this week:

they asked her,

"why are we here at a time when
there is so much misery and despair?"

she responded,

"because you answered the call. the earth signaled for heroes, and the heavens sent forth the ones who were most ready to grow and unleash their unconditional love. you're here to shine the light of your own healing,to offer the world the gift of your balance and peace"

It's up to all of us to become the heroes and, to do so, we need to start with ourselves.

With love and light,
Nora

Forget safety. Live where you fear to live.
Destroy your reputation. Be notorious.

Rumi
translated by Coleman Barks

21

WINDOW OR AISLE SEAT

Dear All,

The most challenging aspect of 2020 for me has been not seeing my aging parents. They are ninety-two and ninety-five years old and live alone in New York City. I have lost many nights of sleep, worrying about their safety and fearing the worst. I spontaneously decided last week to take the risk and fly to New York. It was nerve-racking as well as a logistical nightmare, but I was guided by my intuition that the risk of travel was not as grave as the risk of not seeing them for another unknown period of time.

I boarded the plane looking like a character in a sci-fi movie, wearing a mask and face shield, spraying the surfaces with disinfectant, and obsessively wiping my hands with sanitizer. I looked down at my boarding pass and noticed that I had a window seat. How could that be? I have to sit in an aisle seat! My brain began to react to this "threat," and I could feel myself wanting to "fight" by demanding my seat of choice. But I chose to take a few long deep breaths instead. A few minutes later, I was nestled in my window seat, praying that I would make it for six hours without getting claustrophobic.

After I meditated, I began to relax and reflect. Aisle seats had always afforded me the opportunity to get up, go to the restroom, and/or walk the aisles. I felt safe in my aisle seat. I was not boxed in; I had easy access out. For most of my life, I was perpetually on the go, rarely resting or staying in one place, physically, mentally, or emotionally. Being on the go and getting things done were my trademark.

But in the years since becoming a meditation leader, I have been slowly embracing the beauty in stillness and in the wisdom of "staying," as Pema Chodron calls it.

I did something I had never done before. I lifted the shade and looked out the window. Although I could feel the fear in my body, I took a good look at where I was in the moment, flying above the clouds. I was in flight, traveling from the west coast where I have lived for a decade, and the East Coast where I had lived for half a century—where my parents, siblings, and two of my four children still live.

I welled up with tears. I didn't want to look away anymore—I wanted to be fully present—to what is difficult as well as what is joyous.

A window of opportunity . . . A window into your soul . . . Windows of the world . . . How often we use the analogy to describe a clearing, an opening, a soulful moment or vision.

I needed a window more than I knew.

Dr. Daniel Siegel coined the term, the "window of tolerance," to describe the optimal arousal level of brain/body reactions, suggesting that when we are in that "window of tolerance," we can manage the ebb and flow of our emotions without going into fight, flight, or freeze mode. When we begin to go into a more hyperarousal (anxious) state, meditating and breathing are recommended!

For the first time in my life, I did not get up once during the flight.

I read, wrote, reflected, and looked out the window, committed to seeing the moment, my life, the world as it actually is, with love at its core.

Carl Sandburg expressed it beautifully:

Give me hunger,
O you gods that sit and give
The world its orders.
Give me hunger, pain and want,
Shut me out with shame and failure
From your doors of gold and fame,
Give me your shabbiest, weariest hunger!
But leave me a little love,
A voice to speak to me in the day end,
A hand to touch me in the dark room

BE STILL & SOAR

Breaking the long loneliness.
In the dusk of day-shapes
Blurring the sunset,
One little wandering, western star
Thrust out from the changing shores of shadow.
Let me go to the window,
Watch there the day-shapes of dusk
And wait and know the coming
Of a little love.

      With love and light,
      Nora

Give me hunger,
O you gods that sit and give
The world its orders.
Give me hunger, pain and want,
Shut me out with shame and failure
From your doors of gold and fame,
Give me your shabbiest, weariest hunger!
But leave me a little love,
A voice to speak to me in the day end,
A hand to touch me in the dark room
Breaking the long loneliness.
In the dusk of day-shapes
Blurring the sunset,
One little wandering, western star
Thrust out from the changing shores
of shadow.
Let me go to the window,
Watch there the day-shapes of dusk
And wait and know the coming
Of a little love.

Carl Sandburg

22
THIS TOO...

Dear All,

Does it feel like you are just getting through one challenge, and another is right there waiting for you?

Just when the news couldn't get worse, it does?

Just when you begin to feel like you are grounded, the rug gets pulled out from under you again?

Most of us are feeling waves of loss, fear, restlessness, isolation, and worry which continue to knock us over, day after day, moment after moment.

Our country is in crisis, and many of us are struggling with finances, family issues, physical, and mental issues.

And then, this week one of my closest friends lost a loved one in a tragic hit-and-run accident.

How could that happen, too?

The refrain to the song of our lives right now seems to be "this too?"

How can we take anymore? How can we not rail against what's happening and feel trapped in our despair and disappointment?

Somehow, we have to find equanimity—mental calmness and composure in difficult situations.

Consider this verse from the Theragatha, a Buddhist text, in a translation edited by Anne Bancroft:

> If your mind becomes firm like a rock
> And no longer shakes
> In a world where everything is shaking,
> Your mind will be your greatest friend
> And suffering will not come your way.

We can learn to cultivate this nonjudgmental presence by focusing on the space between the stimulus and our response, which Viktor Frankl says is synonymous with freedom.

Instead of asking the question, "This too?" when hit with a trigger, try just breathing in "this," and releasing "too." "This too" becomes a statement, a mantra, a way of accepting anything and everything that comes at you, rather than questioning/fighting/resisting whatever is happening. "This too?" becomes "This too . . ."

Gandhi took a day off every week to sit and do nothing so that "my actions arise from the wisdom of my heart." That's what we want to move towards—sourcing ourselves in a balanced presence so that our actions can arise from a wisdom that is free from grasping an aversion.

How do we develop equanimity?

1. Embrace our obstacles rather than trying to avoid, control, and manipulate every experience.
2. Bring the qualities of composure and poise to each task.
3. Move your body in mindful ways.
4. Expose yourself to cultures and traditions other than your own.
5. Look out at the horizon as often as you can.
6. Meditate daily.
7. Discover new music.
8. Read inspirational books by people who have traveled this road.
9. When you get triggered, write down your thoughts and feelings, and then acknowledge that you are not your thoughts or feelings.

Equanimity is a conditioned state that resembles the liberated mind. It is not about ignoring the fear, the rage, the doubt, but including it all. When you keep including and allowing everything that is happening, the heart will be ready for anything. From there, we can respond with care.

It is not an easy road to travel, but it is well worth it because, ultimately, we are brought closer to ourselves.

THIS TOO...

Follow the invisible path that brings you out of reactivity to your most awakened self.

Mirabai Starr, in her introduction to her translation of St. Teresa of Avila's *The Interior Castle*, encourages you:

> There is a secret place. A radiant sanctuary. As real as your own kitchen. More real than that. . . .
>
> This magnificent refuge is inside you. Enter. Shatter the darkness that shrouds the doorway. Step around the poisonous vipers that slither at your feet, attempting to throw you off your course. Be bold. Be humble. . . . Close your eyes and follow your breath to the still place that leads to the invisible path that leads you home.

With love and light,
Nora

There is a secret place. A radiant sanctuary. As real as your own kitchen. More real than that. . . .

This magnificent refuge is inside you. Enter. Shatter the darkness that shrouds the doorway. Step around the poisonous vipers that slither at your feet, attempting to throw you off your course. Be bold. Be humble. . . . Close your eyes and follow your breath to the still place that leads to the invisible path that leads you home.

Mirabai Starr

23
LOVE IS THE ANSWER

Dear All,

My dear friend's ex-husband and father of her sons died in a tragic accident last week. I was asked to officiate his Celebration of Life.

I prepared for days, intent on offering the perfect words, playing the perfect music, reciting the perfect poetry.

I wanted the occasion to be authentic, meaningful, inclusive, and inspiring. Hundreds of people joined on Zoom to pay their respects.

In the calm environment, a deep sense of community was created. As at most funerals, there were heartfelt tributes, laughter, and tears.

I brought the group into a momentary meditation, breathing in love and releasing loss, focusing on sending love and support to the family.

When the service was over, I was overcome with emotion.

There was sadness and exhaustion, as well as pride, that it had been so well received.

But there was something more.

The evening had been a demonstration of respect, civility, decency, openness, vulnerability, and support. The atmosphere had been devoid of judgment, cynicism, rancor or dissension.

Everyone was united in love.

I woke up the next morning to the sound of my two-year-old granddaughter giddy with laughter. She ran all over the house, shrieking with delight about everything and nothing. When she snuggled in my lap to hear a story, she was excited, present, and curious. My heart was bursting with joy as I watched my two daughters engage with her. There was nothing but acceptance and warmth.

Everyone was united in love.

It's not surprising that end of life and early life evoke similar emotions.

But can't we summon those sensations more often?

"Love is the only sane and satisfactory answer to the problem of human existence." — *Erich Fromm*

That source of deep love is within us all, waiting and wanting to be accessed.

We can unite in love, no matter the circumstances.

Connect with and invite love in, as often as you can.

See love in the faces of your family and friends. Feel love as you walk on the sand at the beach or as you pet your cat or dog. Hear love when you listen to a favorite piece of music. Experience love in the moments of silence when you are hiking.

It's all around us. Edith Eger, a Holocaust survivor and author of *The Gift*, reminds us that "we're born to love. We learn to hate. It's up to us what we reach for."

Choose love. Reach for love. Express love. Unite in love.

In our broken world, nothing else will work.

In the words of Charles Dickens, "A loving heart is the truest wisdom."

I believe that we all understand in our core that love is transformative and even more so, the only thing that really matters.

When the Beatles' song, "All You Need Is Love," is played, the world seems to listen. There's a soothing quality to it, almost as if we are being reminded that we have what we need and there's no need to search, struggle or grasp for whatever else we think would make us happy. And it's a song that demands to be sung along to, bringing us all into the place where love is truly recognized as the gift it is.

When the world feels disconnected and at odds, I sometimes envision everyone everywhere locking arms, person to person, street to street, city to city, country to country, continent to continent, swaying together and singing at the top of their lungs, willing the power of love to grab hold of the evil and discord and will it away. Who can forget how it felt to watch when singers from around the world came together to sing "We Are the World," demonstrating the healing nature of interconnectedness when we so needed it?

Let's sing together, dance together, share food and traditions, and create the inclusive world we all yearn to belong to.

May we all remember the teaching of His Holiness the Dalai Lama: "Love and compassion are necessities, not luxuries. Without them, humanity cannot survive."

Let's all do our part, and love more and more.

Let's start with ourselves.

With love and light,
Nora

Love is the only sane and satisfactory answer to the problem of human existence.

Erich Fromm

24

TAKE YOUR BROKEN HEART AND TURN IT INTO ART

Dear All,

During the pandemic, it seems like everyone has been experimenting with creative projects. People are knitting, organizing, gardening, crocheting, baking, and then posting their magnificent accomplishments online!

I made one sourdough bread and that was enough.

I don't garden or sew or throw pots.

My husband had a dream that I starting painting and became a successful painter. He bought me a beautiful easel and paints. I have always considered myself the worst painter on the planet, so I haven't opened the paints or set up the easel, and probably never will.

But creativity does not have to be about pushing oneself to make visual art unless that speaks to you. As Mark Nepo says, "Creativity, whatever form it takes, is less about creating something out of nothing and more about being in relationship and conversation with life and the unknown."

When we express, we let out what's in. Creativity is about expression, and all forms of expression are meant to awaken the love that is possible in the world. You simply have to open your heart and let what's there flow. Expression will find you.

How do we ignite our expression?

We are open to everything around us, we listen, taste, touch, smell, and hear.

We all have something in us that's been a thread, a constant in our lives.

This is the theme of William Stafford's poem, "The Way it Is":

> There's a thread you follow. It goes among
> things that change. But it doesn't change.
> People wonder about what you are pursuing.
> You have to explain about the thread.
> But it is hard for others to see.
> While you hold it you can't get lost.
> Tragedies happen; people get hurt
> or die; and you suffer and get old.
> Nothing you do can stop time's unfolding,
> You don't ever let go of the thread.

To discover this thread that goes through everything is the main reason to be curious, use your senses, and notice what lifts you into joy or throws you into sadness of pain.

My form of expression has always been writing.

I've written letters, toasts, stories, summations, briefs, books, memoirs, essays, and speeches.

But never, until last week, had I written a memorial service. The thread was undeniable. I was at my most creative, weaving together the elements of the service, the poems, the songs, the tributes, along with short but powerful meditations, combining them to create a deeply meaningful service.

I felt something I hadn't felt since I was a prosecutor giving my closing arguments.

There was no "I" when I was leading the event—I was in "the zone." It was exactly what D.H. Lawrence meant when he wrote, "Not I, but the wind that blows through me." I completely understood what Steven Nachmanovitch meant when he talked about "the noun of you becoming a verb."

We are shaken, unsure, and anxious. As Carrie Fisher said, "Take your broken heart and turn it into art."

Creativity brings us closer to our true essence. Ask yourself what causes a revolution in your heart? What lifts you up to joy? Where do you feel the greatest pain?

We are all deeply creative people and want to access that creativity, that thread that has been your constant, by opening up to doing what brings you to life, following your fascinations, your obsessions, compulsions.

When we can't take it anymore, we need to get out of our heads, acknowledge our powerlessness but come back to ourselves by creating.

As Elizabeth Gilbert asks in her book, *Big Magic*, "Do you have the courage to bring forth the treasures that are hidden within you?"

Say yes! We need you and your beautiful creative expression!

In *Letters to a Young Poet* (Søren Filipski's translation), Rainer Maria Rilke instructs: "I could give you no advice but this: to go into yourself and to explore the depths whence your life wells forth; at its source you will find the answer to the question whether you must create."

Close your eyes and take three long, slow, deep breaths. Ask yourself this question:

"When I am my most alive?"

Listen carefully.

Find that thread, follow that revolution in your heart, listen to the answer from within.

Dance. Dream. Paint. Crochet. Play music. Whatever it is that brings you from a noun to a verb . . .

Let what's in out.

"You use a glass mirror to see your face: you use works of art to see your soul."

> — *George Bernard Shaw*
> (spoken by a character in the
> play *Back to Methusaleh*)

Bring your soul forth to be seen, appreciated, and loved.

> With love and light,
> *Nora*

Go into yourself and . . . explore the depths whence your life wells forth; at its source you will find the answer to the question whether you must create.

Rainer Maria Rilke
translated by Søren Filipski

25
I'M SHRINKING

Dear All,

What do you think of when you hear the term "Shrinking Violet"?

I imagine a group of beautiful, happy, carefree, and talkative young people enjoying the thrill of a dance or party while a plain, lonely girl stands in a corner—tense, fearful, and unable to interact successfully with the group, shrinking in discomfort.

I have had moments in my life when I have felt like that girl, but never have I felt more like I am shrinking than in these last seven months.

Some of you may wonder why I am talking about shrinking when so many people are talking about gaining the COVID-15, but explore with me whether you can also relate to feeling the sensation of shrinking.

I feel my world is shrinking in every aspect of my life.

I don't see a wide circle of friends or family anymore. My social life is shrinking.

I don't attend concerts, movies, or plays, nor do I go to museums or live events. My cultural life is shrinking.

I'M SHRINKING

I tend to cook a lot of the same dishes, over and over. I don't go out to restaurants to explore new foods and taste sensations. My culinary life is shrinking.

I wear the same five or six comfortable outfits over and over, rarely putting on anything new or particularly fetching. My style life is shrinking.

I no longer go to an office and therefore don't have that put together/bad ass/professional look that was an integral part of me since graduating from law school over thirty years ago. My professional demeanor is shrinking.

I no longer wear high heels, so I am literally shrinking! I look at myself in the mirror and barely recognize myself. I am three to four inches shorter in my slippers. Even my youngest child towers over me.

My body is shrinking.

I can't help but think about Alice in Wonderland, where things are unpredictable and disturbing, and where Alice takes mysterious potions and cakes that give her the ability to grow and shrink on a whim, but never allowing her the power to be the size she needs to be.

In some ways, we are becoming minimalists, getting rid of all the things (and perhaps people) that hold us back, distract us, and confuse us. In that sense, shrinking has value.

We can experience more freedom when we declutter, giving us more time to focus on the most important things and people in life.

But it doesn't mean that experiencing a shrinking life is easy. I miss taking my kids to the theater. I miss going with my husband to our favorite nightspot and listening to live music. I miss getting dressed up and going to work, feeling powerful and relevant.

Sometimes, I feel like the Wicked Witch of the West when the bucket of water is thrown on her and she screams, "I'm melting," as she disappears into nothingness.

But then I recall the book I used to read to my kids called *Papa, Please Get the Moon for Me* by Eric Carle.

The little girl is desperate to play with the moon but it's too big for her father to carry it for her. "Every night I get a little smaller," said the moon. "When I am the right size, you can take me with you." And indeed the moon gets smaller and smaller and smaller until finally her father is able to get it for her. The little girl loves playing, dancing with, and hugging the moon, but it keeps getting smaller and smaller until it finally disappears altogether. Then, one night the little girl sees a thin sliver of the moon reappear. Each night it grows bigger and bigger until it becomes the full moon again.

Maybe our situation is similar—that we need to grow smaller and smaller so that we become more accessible, more easily held and nurtured, and that in time we will again reappear and grow into our most glorious selves.

After all, when we breathe in, our ribs expand and when we exhale, they contract. We shrink on the exhalation, activating our parasympathetic nervous system which allows us to rest and digest.

Maybe that is what we need.

In his book, *Think Like a Monk*, Jay Shetty describes entering the ashram where he is training to be a monk and being led to a dusty storeroom lined with unused books and artifacts, covered with cobwebs. There is a mirror there and he is asked to describe what he sees. Through the thick layer of dust, Jay can't see his own reflection. The senior monk instructs: "Your identity is a mirror covered with dust. When you first look in the mirror, the truth of who you are and what you value is obscured. Clearing it may not be pleasant, but only when that dust is gone can you see your true reflection."

We are clearing away what's unnecessary, so that we can see and be our truest identities.

In cooking, reduction is the process of thickening or intensifying the flavor of a sauce by simmering or boiling until the desired concentration is reached by evaporation. The sauce becomes more flavorful and delicious by shrinking.

We are doing the same.

And as we look out at the world, so many millions of others, all over the globe are experiencing a similar phenomenon. As W.E.B. Du Bois writes, "The world is shrinking together; it is finding itself neighbor to itself in strange, almost magical degrees."

This is a strange time.

But perhaps by dusting off the mirror, by exhaling, reducing, and shrinking, we will become clearer about our values and edge closer to the truth of who we are as individuals and communities. And that would be magic.

With love and light,
Nora

The world is shrinking together; it is finding itself neighbor to itself in strange, almost magical degrees.

W.E.B. Du Bois

26
WHEN WILL THIS BE OVER?

Dear All,

When is this craziness going to end?

It feels like we are being pushed over the edge.

It's been three days, and we don't know who our next President will be.

It is more than anxiety-producing—it's debilitating. We feel anger, fear, overwhelm, and exhaustion.

For many of us, these are not new sensations.

Many of us have experienced burnout at other times in our lives.

Originally defined in 1975, pertaining to the workplace, burnout has three components:

1. Emotional exhaustion
2. Depersonalization, depletion of empathy
3. Decreased sense of accomplishment/feeling like everything is futile and nothing makes a difference

It is the emotional exhaustion that wreaks the most havoc on our bodies.

When I started The Gathering, I was committed to being a source of comfort for women who do too much. I wanted to nurture women who, like me, had spent their lives giving to others.

What has become clearer to me is the emotional and physical toll this over-giving has on women.

In her book, *Down Girl: The Logic of Misogyny*, Kate Manne is of the opinion that there are two types of human beings—human beings whose moral obligation is to be a human being, and human givers whose moral obligation is to give their humanity to human beings, including their time, attention, patience, love, rest, bodies, hopes, and dreams,

Any doubt who the women are? Yes—we are Human Givers!

In their recent book on the subject, *Burnout: The Secret to Unlocking the Stress Cycle*, Emily and Amelia Nagoski suggest that this exhaustion comes when our feelings get caught in our bodies, unable to find their way out. It is up to us to learn how to complete that cycle, freeing us from the choke-hold of stress.

Human Givers (women) burnout from giving too much.

The authors suggest that "we get exhausted and we wonder if we can accomplish any of the things we hope for, without destroying ourselves in the process. We ask ourselves if it's time to quit."

We are exhausted from giving, from hoping, from watching the news, from caring for our families, from working, and from worrying about our country and the world.

We have to look closely and separate the stressors, the things that create the stress, from the stress itself.

We are told that we need to do something to complete the cycle of stress to effectively deal with the overwhelm.

Any one of these will work:

- » PHYSICAL ACTIVITY
- » SLEEP
- » BREATHING
- » IMAGINATION
- » SELF-EXPRESSION
- » CRYING
- » SOCIAL CONNECTION
- » INTIMATE CONNECTION
- » CONNECTION WITH NATURE
- » SPIRITUAL CONNECTION

For my family, CONNECTION was how we dealt with our stress last night.

My dad turned ninety-five years old and we had a Zoom birthday party with his younger brother, my mom, my brother and his husband, my sister, my husband, his six grandchildren, and a few significant others. We sang to him, shared stories, pictures, and poems, and laughed and cried.

My dad has been involved with politics throughout his life. We have campaigned for many candidates, celebrating on some Election Days and licking our wounds on others. My dad taught us to be good sports, tell the truth, and stand up for what's right. I thought a lot about what a great leader he has been in our family and in his professional life.

We honor his honesty, integrity, and loyalty and yearn for a leader with those values.

This is a hard time, but we can learn and grow from the experience.

We need to acknowledge our emotional exhaustion, to complete the stress cycle by breathing, moving, hugging, laughing, connecting, trusting, and crying.

We will get through this time of exhaustion.

We will come through this Year of Burnout.

How? By digging deep, connecting with our values and living from them.

In her newsletter, Maria Shriver, who also has had a lot of ups and downs on Election Days, shares her thoughts about getting through this time: "I'm going to ask my higher self to lead me forward. I need her today. I need her steadiness. I need her wisdom. I need her ability to Rise Above. I need her tenderness. I need the love she has because there is a lot of hate and anger out there. I need her love to help dissolve that hate."

We all need to connect with our best selves, our higher selves and be guided by them.

Maybe we will have a better sense tomorrow about what our future holds.

But no matter what, we have our selves, our truths, our values.

We will not give up. We will forge ahead and live life with honesty, integrity, and openness.

We will conquer hate with love.

We will get through this.

As Robert Frost said, "In three words I can sum up everything I've learned about life. It goes on."

And so it does.

We will prevail.

With love and light,
Nora

In three words I can sum up everything I've learned about life. It goes on.

Robert Frost

27
WHY DON'T WE FEEL ELATED?

Dear All,

We've been on a roller coaster ride these past few weeks.

Election Day came and went with the results unclear, leaving us all in a heightened state of anxiety mixed with despair.

Finally, on Saturday, it was announced that Joe Biden was the winner and that we would be heralding in a new era in American politics!

Why doesn't it feel more celebratory? More definitive?

Perhaps because we have yet to hear the loser concede the election.

Perhaps because, as we have learned, stress doesn't just dissipate when the stressor is removed.

We know that people often sink further into depression immediately after the divorce they initiated is finalized.

We know that almost all students get sick after finally turning in their dissertations.

WHY DON'T WE FEEL ELATED?

We know that a majority of concentration camp survivors were unable to live happy lives after finally being liberated.

It's not always easy to move on.

Even when we've been desperate to move on.

Some people didn't realize that they had been holding their breath for the past few years.

Some people were hoping for a more sweeping victory—a full renunciation of what was—and feel disappointed.

For many of us, we have been in hiding, trying to get through the dark times, and are resistant to coming out yet, unsure of how it will be.

I can remember as a child, playing hide and seek with my siblings, hearing "come out, come out, wherever you are" and wondering if it made more sense to stay in my comfortable, safe hiding place than to come into the harsh light of reality.

Perhaps we should have more compassion for ourselves and think of the hiding, not as cowardly, but as protective.

The poet David Whyte concurs:

> Hiding is a way of staying alive. Hiding is a way of holding ourselves until we are ready to come into the light. Hiding is one of the brilliant and virtuoso practices of almost every part of the natural world:

the protective quiet of an icy northern landscape, the held bud of a future summer rose, the snow-bound internal pulse of the hibernating bear. . . .

Hiding done properly is the internal faithful promise for a proper future emergence.

We may have been hiding because of our fear.
We may have been hiding because of our anger.
We may have been hiding because of our disbelief.
We have allowed something outside of ourselves to take over our time, our hearts, our minds.

In that space of worry, even if we have been actively fighting, there has not been a focus on our inner selves. We have used these years, this hostility, in part to avoid looking inside.

But now is the time to come forth, to emerge.

Who will we be as we emerge?

What have we learned from our hiding and what will we share with others moving forward?

As we emerge, coming into the light, what is the future we want to create?

"The pessimist complains about the wind, the optimist expects it to change; the realist adjusts the sails." — William Arthur Ward.

We are where we are. We have a new leader and a still-divided country.

It's time to be fully present, adjust the sails and move forward.

Go inside and make the adjustments you need to make.

The transformation of the world begins with each one of us.

Listen to the wisdom of the poet Yung Pueblo:

peaceful minds
have the power
to create
a peaceful world

There is much healing to be done, individually and collectively.

Let's begin by taking a very long, slow, deep breath, breathing in right and breathing out now. RIGHT NOW is our time.

Time to cultivate the traits we hope to see in others, to treat others as we want others to treat us. To practice peace.

Do something kind today.

Be compassionate today.

Love someone today.

Forgive someone today.

Speak the truth today.

Even the smallest shift will have an impact.

As Leo Tolstoy says, "True life is lived when tiny changes occur."

Let's all work on making tiny changes in our own minds and our own lives.

And then perhaps we will see the major change we want to see.

With love and light,
Nora

peaceful minds
have the power
to create
a peaceful world

Yung Pueblo

28
SHAKE IT OFF

Dear All,

Do you remember freeze tag, or the cooler version, freeze dance?

It was a staple in our repertoire of games growing up!

I can still feel the sensation of trying to hold my body completely still, willing myself to stay in whatever position I was in when the word "freeze" was announced, hoping against hope that I wouldn't slip up and make any motion whatsoever.

The stakes were high—you were "out" if you were caught moving in even the tiniest way.

Most of you have heard of "fight or flight."

It's how our ancient brains are programmed to respond to a threat, such as an attack by a tiger.

Freeze is the third automatic response to overwhelming danger, whether real or perceived.

The brain turns on the freeze response when fighting or fleeing seem impossible.

Effective self-preservation is one of the positive consequences of the freeze response. In the natural world,

SHAKE IT OFF

animals sometimes play dead so brilliantly that their predators give up and leave before the animal playing dead pops back up and runs off free.

A phenomenon often occurs during a bull fight when the bull retreats into a spot in the ring, and "freezes." This place of refuge is called the querencia, and is considered a place of stillness and safety where the bull goes to draw strength.

But freezing can also be a way of avoiding or dreading something, and then our bodies stiffen and our minds become numb, detached, or disassociated.

Freeze can be paralyzing or a saving grace.

We have all experienced moments in our lives when our fear, exhaustion, overwhelm, shock, or disappointment gets the better of us and we find ourselves unable to keep going, resorting to some sort of a freeze response.

How do we thaw?

We can look again at our animal friends. After a gazelle freezes in response to a lion attack and the lion wanders off, something magical happens. Once the threat is gone, the gazelle begins to shake and shudder. All the adrenaline and cortisol that had built up, resulting in the freeze response, get purged and the gazelle returns to herself.

For me, the song "Jump" by the Pointer Sisters had a "thawing" effect on me. If I was frozen in my own self-doubt or self-pity and heard that song on the radio, I would automatically jump up and dance with abandon until I returned to myself. I must have heard, whispered into my ear, the famous words attributed to Rumi: "Dance until you shatter yourself."

Taylor Swift sings about how when she is barraged with negative comments from all sides, she needs to "shake it off, shake it off" so that she can unfreeze herself and move on.

Engaging the body is the surest way of breaking out of the freeze cycle. The best thing to do is to pat your legs, stomp your feet, wave your arms, laugh if you can. Walk, run, do yoga, surf. Movement sends a message to the brain that you are safe.

Joe Biden shook himself out of the freeze response when he jogged, instead of walked, out to the podium to give his acceptance speech last week. I could feel him breaking out of the stuck position he had been in all week, finally able to reclaim his power.

Many of us have felt frozen these last months—worried, fearful, anxious, angry.

Remember the bull is his strongest, most powerful self when he emerges from his querencia.

We freeze from fear, from sadness, from loss.

And then we thaw and experience joy and rebirth.

It's time to thaw out, to jump, jog, shake it off.

We need you to get back to you.

Be your most powerful, effective, loving, and strong self.

You've played dead long enough. The predator is gone. Shake, shudder, and run gracefully into your life.

Because, as Joseph Campbell says, "The privilege of a lifetime is being who you are."

Be her.

With love and light,
Nora

The privilege of a lifetime
is being who you are.

Joseph Campbell

29
THANK THE GIVERS

Dear All,

The word gratitude is having its day. We are constantly being reminded to be grateful for what we have and to keep a gratitude journal.

Today, many of us went around the Thanksgiving table, sharing what we give thanks for.

As the saying goes, some happy people are grateful, but all grateful people are happy.

And it's all true! Gratitude works.

I am grateful for all the people in my life who have been there for me during difficult times, particularly my friends.

"At times our own light goes out and is rekindled by a spark from another person. Each of us has cause to think with deep gratitude of those who have lighted the flame within us."

Heed the advice of Albert Schweitzer and thank those people around you have have rekindled the spark within you.

I also give thanks to all the people who have brought me happiness, particularly my children. As Marcel Proust says (in Edward Ousselin's translation): "Let us be thankful to people who give us happiness; they are the charming gardeners who make our souls bloom."

May we all have charming gardeners in our lives to nourish us and bring us happiness.

But, in addition to giving thanks, I want to thank the givers.

My purpose in life is to nurture women who give constantly to others, often forgetting to care for themselves. I thank all of you givers, who extend yourselves every day to make sure everyone around you is fed, washed, clothed, educated, organized, happy, and more.

Women are the unsung heroes of this pandemic, making sure that their work lives and home lives, as well as the lives of those around them, are all running smoothly, no matter the toll on their well-being.

Remember to continue to practice gratitude, because "when a person doesn't have gratitude, something is missing in his or her humanity." — *Elie Weisel.*

With love and light,
Nora

Let us be thankful to people who give us happiness; they are the charming gardeners who make our souls bloom.

Marcel Proust
translated by Edward Ousselin

30

WHAT YOU DON'T APPRECIATE, DEPRECIATES

Dear All,

We all know how important it is to incorporate a gratitude practice into our lives.

While gratitude is a feeling, appreciation is an expression.

It is even more important to take the time to appreciate the things, people, and situations in our lives. What we don't appreciate, depreciates.

We rarely make efforts to appreciate our own accomplishments, actions and personality traits. According to William James, "The deepest principle in human nature is the craving to be appreciated."

It's not surprising that most of us feel unappreciated in our homes, with our families, and on our jobs. By appreciating ourselves more, we could change that.

The challenge is that we are more likely to see what's wrong with ourselves than to acknowledge and appreciate our own talents and strengths.

WHAT YOU DON'T APPRECIATE, DEPRECIATES

"Most of the shadows of life are caused by standing in one's own sunshine." — *Ralph Waldo Emerson*

While it is true that we are responsible for stepping out of the shadows and standing in our own sunshine, it is a tall order.

How do we undo years of doubting ourselves, criticizing ourselves, talking negatively about ourselves, and devaluing ourselves?

For most of us, the focus on our weaknesses feels automatic.

In my training as a lawyer, I was taught to see the flaws in every case and that "skill" has become ingrained in me. I know exactly where I need to improve, but am often unable to see or appreciate where I excel.

How do we become more appreciative of our strengths?

One way is to follow the wisdom of Sister Joan Chittister, a Benedictine monk, who wrote: "It is trust in the limits of self that makes us open and it is trust in the gifts of others that make us secure. We realize that we don't have to do everything, that we can't do everything and that what I can't do is someone else's gift and responsibility. . . . My limitations make space for the gifts of other people."

What a fantastic new perspective! If we could think of our limitations as other people's gifts, perhaps we could lighten up on ourselves and actually appreciate our strengths.

Rather than being down on myself for not being more organized with all the paper in my office, what if I could consider that organization is someone else's gift and let my disappointment in my lack go?

Instead of focusing on our weaknesses, we could lean into our strengths and make ways to make them central in our lives.

It's time to consider the possibility that we really can free ourselves from judgment and criticism, and learn to deeply appreciate ourselves.

Ask yourself, where how you been undervaluing yourself?

Where haven't you been appreciating yourself?

Allow yourself to have a subtle shift in outlook, to become more appreciative.

"The real voyage of discovery consists not of seeking new landscapes, but of having new eyes." — Marcel Proust

Remember to view your limitations as someone else's gift.

Look with new eyes and see the magnificence of you.

I appreciate you. Make sure you do, too.

With love and light,
Nora

Most of the shadows of life
are caused by standing in
one's own sunshine.

Ralph Waldo Emerson

31
WHAT IS HUMBLE PIE?

Dear All,

I never really understood what it meant when someone was told to eat humble pie.

Although I knew it was an admonition to stop bragging, it wasn't until recently, while studying ancient spiritual teachers, that I gained a deeper understanding of the true lessons in humility.

The ego is two-faced. One moment it tells us we are great at everything, and the next moment it tells us we're the worst. Either way we are blind to the reality of who we really are. True humility is seeing what lies between the extremes.

Instead of allowing the ego's all-or-nothing way of being, humility allows us to understand our weaknesses and want to improve, not to give up on ourselves or get into self-loathing or self-criticism.

Lord Brahma, the god of Creation, apologized to Krishna, the Supreme god, because in the course of building the world, he was too impressed with himself. He confessed that he was like a firefly. At night, when a

WHAT IS HUMBLE PIE?

firefly glows, it thinks how bright I am, how amazing, I'm lighting up the whole sky. But in the light of day, no matter how brightly the firefly glows, its light is weak, if not invisible, and it realizes its insignificance. Brahma thought he was lighting the world, but when the sun came out he was just a firefly.

In the darkness of the ego, we think we're special and powerful and significant, but when we look at ourselves in context of the great universe, we see how tiny a part we play.

Perhaps the reason why I never grappled with humility was that I had the most incredible role model in the world.

My dad—an incredibly successful, brilliant, and talented man—always led by example. He has always been authentically humble, never once seeing himself as better than anyone else. He's the guy who feels as connected to the doormen in his building as with the men and women with whom he served in John F. Kennedy's administration.

Ralph Waldo Emerson wrote, "A great man is always willing to be little," and that was what was modeled to us.

Not being arrogant was a given. But there's another lesson in humility that I didn't know I had also been taught.

Focusing on our own insecurities, failures, and self-doubt is just as much a function of the ego as is bragging and self-aggrandizing.

Why? Because when we feel insecure, worried that we are not where we want to be in our careers or relationships, our self-esteem plummets. This is also solely about us.

As Thomas Moore says in *Care of the Soul*, "Being literally undone by failure is akin to 'negative narcissism.'"

We need to appreciate failure with imagination and reconnect it to success, or it falls into narcissistic fantasies of success and dismal feelings of failure.

To be humble we need to be neither hindered by self-doubt and criticism nor blinded by arrogance and self-centeredness.

I did not realize that my self-doubt, negative self-talk, and fear of failure have made me less humble.

> "True humility is not thinking less of yourself. It is thinking of yourself less." — *Rick Warren*

Yet, as I think about it, it makes sense that those traits are another way of not living our most authentic selves and keep us from being available to serve others in the most humble way.

WHAT IS HUMBLE PIE?

As I think about my dad, I realize that although I have never once heard him brag, nor did I ever hear him put himself down.

He never obsessed about what he didn't achieve or where he slipped up. He didn't seem troubled by his failings.

His successes were no more or less important than his challenges. He was always steady, focused, and humble.

Radhanath Swami talks about the qualities we need for self-actualization, and suggests that we need to be like salt—only noticed when there is too much or not enough.

When salt is used in the best way possible, it goes unrecognized. Salt is so humble that when something goes wrong, it takes the blame. When everything goes right, it doesn't take the credit.

Sounds a lot like my dad.

I will continue learning.

If you are inspired to become more humble, Mother Teresa offers some tips on ways to practice humility:

Mind one's own business.
Accept contradictions and correction cheerfully.
Pass over the mistakes of others.
Accept insults, being slighted, forgotten or disliked.
Be kind and gentle, even under provocation.Choose always what is hardest.

We are all works in progress and growth is our only teacher.

As W. L. Sheldon wrote, "There is nothing noble in being superior to some other man. The true nobility is in being superior to your previous self."

May you grow and become superior only to your previous self.

With love and light,
Nora

True humility is not thinking less of yourself. It is thinking of yourself less.

Rick Warren

32
OUR NEED FOR BELONGING

Dear All,

December is traditionally a month of celebrations, family gatherings, and feelings of belonging.

This year is different.

We are likely not with our extended families or our children who live out of town.

There's a gloominess to this year's holidays, but also a sense of deep gratitude if we are healthy and working, as opposed to so many of our friends and neighbors, who are experiencing illness, financial insecurity and loss.

It's not easy to acknowledge our feelings of disconnectedness, especially now.

Meghan Markle wrote an op-ed in the *New York Times*, which focused on the need to ask each other the simple question—How are you really?

In the "Tiny Loves" section of the *Sunday Times*, a young woman wrote:

> When my friends ask me over FaceTime how I'm doing, I tell them that I spend a lot of time crying.

It's easier than admitting that I can't seem to get out of bed before two p.m. Or wash the dishes that are stinking up my sink. Or get done any work that I normally love doing. But it's more honest than "good." Sometimes they laugh and say, "Same," and sometimes they look down and I don't know what to say.

The rest of the conversation limps along. I apologize for being a stranger. They call me every week anyway.

These are challenging times, even if we are lucky enough to have homes, jobs, and our health.

We yearn to gather, to hug, to feel that glorious feeling of belonging.

We long to belong because we've tasted it . . . We've been with someone we love, had a feeling of gratitude, stood in wonder at some amazing event in nature, or felt a moment of compassion towards another person. We've felt what belonging feels like and we want more of it.

It feels like safety. Like love.

The urge for belonging is fundamental, and yet we allow ourselves to feel separate.

We need to trust our innate belonging.

When we feel it, there's nothing out there that threatens us.

When we feel at home with our inner life, our actual world can be at peace.

John O'Donohue, the great Irish poet and philosopher, reminds us: "Our bodies know that they belong; it is our minds that make our lives so homeless."

To become more in touch with our belonging, we need to become more aware of our bodies.

The way to confront the fear of not belonging is to drop down from the brain into the heart, where love is always present.

In the words of Swami Maharaj, "The mind creates the abyss, the heart crosses it."

It's all about love. And connectedness. And presence.

Over a year ago, I started The Gathering to bring women together, to create connections with one another while meditating, doing yoga, writing, eating, drinking, laughing, and just being real. I wanted to provide a place of love and belonging.

Who knew that 2020 would shake us to the core, challenge us in almost every area of our lives?

We need to be good to one another these days by asking open-ended questions, listening deeply, and being empathetic.

And we need to continue to gather in new ways.

OUR NEED FOR BELONGING

In her book, *The Art of Gathering*, Priya Parker offers simple, thoughtful ways to create gatherings, in whatever format, that are meaningful and satisfying.

What could we have more of if we made getting together intentional?

Gatherings are to authentically connect, whether we are together in person, on the phone, or on Zoom.

Parker writes that gatherings "crackle and flourish when real thought goes into them, when (often invisible) structure is baked into them, and when a host has the curiosity, generosity, and willingness of spirit to try."

The other night I hosted my company's holiday party on Zoom. Our employees were not particularly interested in the event, assuming it would be stilted, forced, and a bit stupid.

With thought and intention, I was able to create an event that exceeded their expectations. I played music while everyone came on, we played a game that required interaction and, most importantly, I started with a clear intention that the evening was designed to create a sense of connection and a spirit of fun and lightheartedness. And that's what happened.

Gatherings can help us.

Intentional gatherings can save us.

We can create a sense of belonging by being present, focusing on others, appreciating what we have, and letting our hearts open fully.

Make your holiday gatherings meaningful and special by being intentional, no matter where they are or who they are with!

And enjoy them fully because gatherings matter deeply.

When we gather, we can cultivate that sense of belonging.

With love and light,
Nora

Our bodies know that they belong;
it is our minds that make our
lives so homeless.

John O'Donohue

33
OPEN THE DOORS WITHIN US

Dear All,

The last day of 2020 is finally here.

We survived. We made it. We got through it.

It was a year of breaking down—our routines, our traditions, our sense of safety, and life as we knew it.

But with all the trauma, exhaustion, uncertainty, anxiety, and loss, it was still a year of living.

We ate, slept, read, watched TV, cooked, talked, walked, and worked. We maintained relationships and friendships, developed new ones, and let go of less important ones. We cried and screamed and hugged and prayed.

Isn't that what makes up every year?

I grew up listening to my mother, a Virginia Woolf scholar, talk about "moments of being"—those moments in which an individual experiences a sense of reality, in contrast to the states of "non-being" that dominate most of an individual's conscious life, in which they are separated from reality by a protective covering.

This was a year that left us without our protective covering, and thus more likely to experience these real and very poignant moments.

Moments of being, I was taught, could be the result of shock, discovery, or revelation. Or just an experience that moved us to feel.

In 2020, we experienced moments that ripped us open and moments that filled us with warmth.

Let's reflect on those moments of being in all our lives—the magnificent and the heartbreaking.

As Jonathan Safran Foer said, "You cannot protect yourself from sadness without protecting yourself from happiness."

So why try to protect ourselves at all?

We have learned to be open to what matters and, in our raw and unprotected state, we have been able to hold on simultaneously to the tragic as well as the cherished moments.

A phone call from an old friend, a baby's first words, the comfort of a loved one, an uncontrollable laugh about nothing, seeing a parent for the first time in months, holding hands while watching the news and fearing the worst, a long walk on the beach, a college graduation, or a birthday on Zoom.

These moments of being make up every year.

We learn from Abraham Joshua Heschel that "the higher goal of spiritual living is not to amass a wealth of information, but to face sacred moments" — to turn toward, not away from, the life we already have.

It is in opening the doors to ourselves, to our existing lives—flawed, imperfect, challenged, disappointing, abundant, and glorious—and embracing all the moments of being, seeing them as sacred, and allowing them to have an impact on our soul, that gives our lives meaning.

So, although everyone may be making ridiculous New Year's resolutions to work out more, lose weight, and organize closets, you don't have to.

We are talking about moments of BE-ing.

You don't have to DO anything.

There is value, however, in giving thought to who you want to BE as we begin the New Year.

As I contemplate who I want to be in 2021, I recall my favorite Maya Angelou quote: "I've learned that people will forget what you said, they will forget what you did, but people will never forget how you made them feel."

I enter this New Year with a commitment to make the people around me, both near and far, those new and old relationships, at work and at home, feel loved and supported.

With love and light,
Nora

> You cannot protect
> yourself from sadness
> without protecting
> yourself from happiness.
>
> *Jonathan Safran Foer*

34
THE WEIGHT OF WAITING

Dear All,

"And now let us believe in a long year that is given to us, new, untouched, full of things that have never been. . . ." — *Rainer Maria Rilke* (in a letter dated January 1, 1907)

We have already seen that 2021 will be filled with new (and still challenging) things, but can we please take a moment to acknowledge getting through 2020, a year which many of us will remember as one of the worst years of our lives?!

We survived, which on its own is a huge accomplishment.

I hope you give yourselves some props.

Despite the challenges of fatigue, depression, boredom, illness, loss, confusion, and uncertainty, you did it.

You demonstrated grit, resilience, steadfastness, and a determination to develop new perspectives, reevaluate many stale beliefs, and live life with a new awareness.

We may have battle scars, but we are still standing.

In many respects, 2020 was about waiting—waiting for information about COVID-19, waiting for lockdown to be over, for our kids to go back to school, waiting for the election results, waiting for the vaccine to be discovered and administered.

We spent a year waiting.

Waiting has allowed us to put off making decisions on where we want to live, whether to stay in or leave relationships, whether to change jobs or careers, or what to do next with our lives.

We are waiting to express ourselves, come back to life, experience rejoicing.

We may be waiting to clarify who we are and what matters most.

Waiting has weighed us down.

However, not everything about waiting has been negative. We've developed patience, become more comfortable with slowing down, and accepting of having fewer answers.

The question now is: Is it time to stop waiting?

Is it time to consider why you may be waiting to do what you want to do or be, or who you want to be?

I think of the opening of the poem "Waiting" by Leza Lowitz: "You keep waiting for something to happen / the thing that lifts you out of yourself . . ."

But actually, life is still moving; nothing has stopped.

Let's seize the moment and be aware, as Ralph Waldo Emerson is, of "how much of human life is lost in waiting."

2020 did certainly feel like an agonizing amount of lost time this year.

But we've stepped in to 2021.

What are you longing for this year?

Who do you want to be?

Is there something specific you are waiting to do, but you worry you are not ready to do?

Heed the advice from the children's book *Lemony Snicket:*

> "Are you ready?" Klaus asked finally.
>
> "No," Sunny answered.
>
> "Me neither," Violet said, "but if we wait until we're ready we'll be waiting for the rest of our lives. Let's go."

Take a little time to think about what you fear you are not ready for.

Are we ever really ready for anything?

I am reading Barack Obama's new book, *A Promised Land*. He brilliantly and elegantly writes about knowing when to wait and when to go for it. He almost didn't run for President because he wasn't ready.

He wisely reminds us, "Change will not come if we wait for some other person or some other time. We are the ones we've been waiting for. We are the change that we seek."

As Anne Frank is quoted as saying, "How wonderful it is that nobody need wait a single moment before starting to improve the world."

I would add "or one's self."

I hereby vow to stop waiting!

I won't wait a single moment more before starting to improve the world. And myself.

Join me if it feels right.

It will be worth the wait.

With love and light,
Nora

Change will not come if we wait for some other person or some other time. We are the ones we've been waiting for. We are the change that we seek.

Barack Obama

35

IS SELF-COMPASSION SELFISH?

Dear All,

What do you think of when you hear the word self-compassion?

For me, I hear self-indulgence, mixed in with a bit of woo-woo.

Some of you may love the word and be fully committed to the practice of self-compassion.

Good for you!

But many of us have a less evolved relationship with self-compassion.

Maybe we don't think we deserve it or that it has to be earned. Maybe we associate it with people who are selfish or shallow.

And maybe we have no idea what it really means.

I've spent most of my adult life taking care of others, and have given almost no thought to what it would look or feel like to be good to myself..

Something feels distant about self-compassion for me.

Desirable, yet distant.

But the more I coach women to slow down and take better care of themselves, the more I realize that I've got my own work to do in this arena.

I thought that Louise Hay was talking to me personally in her quote: "You have been criticizing yourself for years, and it hasn't worked. Try approving of yourself and see what happens."

We are so hard on ourselves.

We ruminate relentlessly about what we did wrong, what we messed up, what we might have done differently.

While all of you who read this book are deeply compassionate human beings, you may find it challenging to turn that warm, giving compassionate-self inward.

As meditation teacher and author, Jack Kornfeld, teaches: "If your compassion does not include yourself, it is incomplete."

So, let's look at how we can tame our inner critic and become more compassionate to ourselves.

Chris Germer, the co-founder of the Center for Mindful Self-Compassion, promises that it's easier than we think. He says, "Self-compassion is simply giving the same kindness towards ourselves that we would give to others."

We need to become better friends with ourselves so that we can be better friends to those around us and expand the circle of tolerance, love, and acceptance.

IS SELF-COMPASSION SELFISH?

To the extent we make headway individually, we will make headway in the world.

It's important to sit in meditation, do no harm, expand our own awareness and awareness of the world, bringing in compassion and wisdom. The whole purpose of meditation is to connect more deeply—to ourselves and ultimately to the world. We need to pay more attention, see things more clearly so that we can take thoughtful and meaningful actions to repair the world.

We want to expand, rather than be limited by, our small, self-critical minds so that we can include other ways of viewing the world.

The poet Yung Pueblo reminds us:

> the beauty
> of self-love
> is that it can
> grow into the
> unconditional love
> that can end all harm

So, we do need to keep leaning towards self-compassion and self-love, if only to save the world from hate and intolerance.

The scientific research is clear that self-compassion really changes our brain so that we can be more effective, productive, and focused.

Let's consider how to give ourselves the nurturing, encouragement, and support that we give our children, our friends, our colleagues.

The three components of self-compassion:

1. Kindness towards yourself: Make an effort to offer yourself a bit of warmth, a little tenderness in those moments of doubt, failure, frustration, and self-criticism. Imagine how you would treat a friend going through the same thing.

2. Common humanity: Remember that whatever you are feeling in the moment, countless others have experienced the same doubt, failure or disappointment, so you are in good company.

3. Mindfulness: Breathing centers you so that you can listen to your inner voice, rather than the inner critic. Remember that you are not your thoughts—particularly the negative, self-critical ones.

Another tip I give to my private clients is to give your inner critic a name. When she starts going on and on about what you didn't do or could have done better or what a loser you are, thank her for sharing and move on. It may sound silly, but the more you separate yourself from your inner critic, the less you will identify with her. Tell her to leave you alone!

IS SELF-COMPASSION SELFISH?

It turns out that self-compassion is actually essential.

The Dalai Lama says, "Love and compassion are necessities, not luxuries. Without them, humanity cannot survive."

Let's bring on the compassion both for ourselves and others.

The world has never needed it more.

This poem, "Love after Love" by Derek Walcott, is a beautiful homage to self-compassion.

> The time will come
> when with elation
> you will greet yourself arriving
> at your own door, in your own mirror
> and each will smile at the other's welcome,
>
> and say, sit here. Eat.
> You will love again the stranger who was your self.
> Give wine. Give bread. Give back your heart
> to itself, to the stranger who has loved you
>
> all your life, whom you ignored
> for another, who knows you by heart.
> Take down the love letters from the bookshelf,
>
> the photographs, the desperate notes,
> peel your own image from the mirror
> Sit. Feast on your life.

Great reminder to "feast on your life."
Sending love to all.

With love and light,
Nora

the beauty
of self-love
is that it can
grow into the
unconditional love
that can end all harm

Yung Pueblo

36
THE IMPORTANCE OF A "TRUST FUND"

Dear All,

The first few weeks of 2021 have been wild.

An insurrection, an impeachment, and an inauguration.

This week finally offered us a sense of relief and we all collectively exhaled.

Some of us didn't even realize how long we had been holding our breath.

This year has challenged us in so many ways, shaking our trust to its core.

We've had to examine long-held beliefs and question life as we've known it.

We are wearing masks, unable to see each other, or be fully seen.

Our trust in the government, the economy, and our health care system has been rattled.

Worried about COVID—it's hard to trust anyone.

Let's examine the nature of trust a bit.

THE IMPORTANCE OF A "TRUST FUND"

If you've had a baby or you've watched a baby with its mother, you know exactly what trust is, although you might not be able to find the words to accurately express what it looks or feels like. Babies trust that they will be cared for; mothers trust the connection to their child will be unlike any other in their lives.

There's nothing quite like feeling or even witnessing that unwavering trust.

When we connect with the experience of trust, we want to trust more.

Trust begets trust.

Unfortunately, most of us formed less than perfect relationships with trust in our early years.

Trust is a triggering word of most of us.

Some trust blindly, some of us never trust, but we all struggle in one way or another with trust.

I know for me there was a time I gave someone my complete trust, changed my entire life based on promises that person made, and ultimately was betrayed.

When we experience that break in trust, it is often hard, or for some it feels impossible, to open our hearts to trust again.

And yet, it's a conundrum because it's the opening up, the loving again that actually brings us back to ourselves, able to trust again.

The author George Eliot writes: "What loneliness is more lonely than distrust?"

When you feel those waves of distrust, don't you also feel a deep loneliness?

The Tao Te Ching tells us (as translated by Gia-fu Feng and Jane English), "He who does not trust enough will not be trusted."

Again, the circular nature of trust—how do we become more trusting so as to be more trusted?

We must have trust in order to trust.

How do we do that?

We start with ourselves.

In the words of the great thinker Johann Wolfgang von Goethe: "As soon as you trust yourself, you will know how to live."

Trusting oneself is not about trusting that we will do everything perfectly, make the best decisions, choose the right people or paths.

It's simply about trusting that no matter what life throws us, we will be able to handle it with a little grace, acceptance, and as much calm as we can muster.

This is exactly what meditation has taught me—to trust that I will be able to face whatever there is to face, by accepting what is and surrendering to the present.

Not easy but it's really our only path to a happy life.

THE IMPORTANCE OF A "TRUST FUND"

We need to believe without evidence, particularly challenging for those of us who are lawyers.

The movie *Field of Dreams* is a great example of allowing in trust.

A corn farmer in Iowa, Ray Kinsella, hears a mysterious voice one night in his cornfield urging him to build a baseball diamond in his cornfields, saying, "If you build it, he will come." Although he wrestles with the decision, he trusts something in himself enough to stake his farm and livelihood on fulfilling his dream and building a baseball field.

We can become more open to trust by connecting to our own still small voice.

Nature is a great teacher in the work of trust.

We trust that the sun will rise in the morning.

We trust that the sun will set in the evening.

And we trust that even when we look up at the sky on a cloudy night, the stars are there, whether we see them or not.

I felt that deep trust begin to bubble up inside me when Amanda Gorman recited her poem at the inauguration. Her words smashed my walls of cynicism and fear, and allowed hope to find its way back. With her poetic words "in this faith we trust," she spoke to the truth that living with trust is a choice.

We need to go inside, listen to our own wisdom, and be guided.

We need to trust.

We know that night will always yield to day. As Gorman said:

> The new dawn blooms as we free it,
> For there is always light,
> If only we're brave enough to see it,
> If only we're brave enough to be it.

Let's trust ourselves, each other, and our communities.

Let's look up at the sky and feel the presence of the magnificent stars, even when they aren't visible. Let's be brave enough to see the light. And to be the light.

With love and light,
Nora

As soon as you trust
yourself, you will know
how to live.

Johann Wolfgang von Goethe

37

TO EVERYTHING THERE IS A SEASON

Dear All,

Last week felt like the beginning of a new season!

The country heralded in a new president amidst music, poetry, love, and calls for unity and truth.

But some change is slower to arrive.

Many of us are still in our winter season, physically and metaphorically.

On the day of the inauguration, I wanted to spend hours curled up on the couch soaking in the positive energy of the day, allowing trust to infiltrate my being, hope to charge me up, and relief to quiet me.

Instead, I was on the phone for hours with my siblings and my mom as my dad was taken to the hospital, having endured another fall.

Euphoria was on the screen, and fear and despair were filling my heart.

Isn't that just the way life is?

As we are celebrating one thing, we are often mourning another.

When one challenge in our life gets resolved, another appears.

But this year has been unique.

For many of us it has been an avalanche of difficulties, one coming right after another, with fewer ups than downs.

Katherine May, in her book *Wintering: The Power of Rest and Retreat in Difficult Times*, describes this period of darkness, which we all experience at different points in our lives.

> Wintering is a season in the cold. It is a fallow period in life when you're cut off from the world, feeling rejected, sidelined, blocked from progress, or cast into the role of an outsider. Perhaps it results from an of illness or a life event such as a bereavement or the birth of a child; perhaps it comes from a humiliation or a failure. Perhaps you're in a period of transition and have temporarily fallen between two worlds. Some winterings creep upon us more slowly, accompanying the protracted death of a relationship, the gradual ratcheting up of caring responsibilities as our parents age, the drip-drip-drip of lost confidence. Some are appallingly sudden, like discovering one day that your skills are considered obsolete, the company you worked for has gone bankrupt, or your partner is in love with

someone new. However it arrives, wintering is usually involuntary, lonely, and deeply painful.

Through her own experience, the author concludes that wintering calls us to slow down and take a closer look at ourselves and our lives, which we can only do while we are in the dark—even when the change is "appallingly sudden," like an unforeseen pandemic.

We are constantly being reminded that it is our struggles that lead us to who we are, that what doesn't kill us makes us stronger, but the focus is usually on when we come out of the difficulty or challenge and can look back on what we learned.

Katherine May brings attention to the intrinsic value of the cold and the darkness itself, writing:

> In our relentlessly busy contemporary world, we are forever trying to defer the onset of winter. We don't ever dare to feel its full bite, and we don't dare to show the way it ravages us. An occasional sharp wintering would do us good. We must stop believing that these times in our lives are somehow silly, a failure of nerve, a lack of willpower. We must stop trying to ignore them or dispose of them. They are real and they are asking something of us. We must learn to invite the winter in. We may never choose to winter, but we can choose how.

Her words resonate so beautifully with all I have learned through my darkest times to the present.

My meditation practice and work as a clarity coach perfectly mirror the insights and lessons in the book.

Ultimately, we want to learn to be in the present, no matter what is happening to and around us, even when it is hard—especially when its hard.

The darkness really is a worthy teacher.

Pema Chodron leads us to the same wisdom: "Things falling apart is a kind of testing and also a kind of healing. We think that the point is to pass the test or overcome the problem, but the truth is that things don't really get solved. They come together and they fall apart. Then they come together and fall apart. It's just like that. The healing comes from letting there be room for all this to happen; room for grief, for relief, for misery, for joy."

This week has seen a lot of rain in Los Angeles and it has been unusually cold. Night seems to arrive in the afternoon. I have a consistent chill and can't be in the house without lighting a fire. It feels like winter for sure.

Katherine May reminds us that "winter is a time of withdrawing from the world, maximizing scant resources, carrying out acts of brutal efficiency and vanishing from sight; but that's where the transformation occurs. Winter is not the death of the life cycle, but its crucible."

Take the time you need to be alone, contemplate, cry, write, stare into space.

Don't try to get past it. Sink into it and trust that there is something to be revealed.

I agree with what Katherine May describes as

"a time of reflection and recuperation, for slow replenishment, for putting your house in order.

Doing these unfashionable things—slowing down, letting your spare time expand, getting enough sleep, resting—is a radical act now, but it is essential. This is a crossroads we all know, a moment when you need to shed a skin. If you do, you'll expose all those painful nerve endings and feel so raw that you'll need to take care of yourself for a while. If you don't then that skin will harden around you."

Maybe I will allow myself time to take a nap in the middle of the day.

A radical act, for sure.

But perhaps not doing so would yield more harmful results.

Staying calm, grounded, and present is what is required.

TO EVERYTHING THERE IS A SEASON

As Yung Pueblo reminds us:

progress is being aware when there
is a storm happening inside you
and remaining calm as it passes by

There will always be storms, coldness, darkness.

And we can weather them all with presence.

I urge you to meditate, reflect, share, and do a little writing.

It's an opportunity not unlike Wintering. We need to slow down, contemplate, connect, and focus on being present.

And yes, the seasons will of course change and the warmth of the sun will feel incredible once again.

When Amanda Gorman read her poem at the inauguration, it was like hearing the chirping of the birds that signal that spring is coming.

Truth, beauty, and the road back to joy are emerging.

What is emerging for you?

With love and light,
Nora

Wintering is a season in the cold. It is a fallow period in life when you're cut off from the world, feeling rejected, sidelined, blocked from progress, or cast into the role of an outsider. Perhaps it results from an illness or a life event such as a bereavement or the birth of a child; perhaps it comes from a humiliation or a failure.

Katherine May

38

A ROOM OF ONE'S OWN

Dear All,

Virginia Woolf's extended essay, "A Room of One's Own," in which she argues that women need to be able to have their own space, unhindered by interruptions, so as to have the intellectual freedom to write is considered a landmark of twentieth century feminist thought.

Here we are almost one hundred years later and women are still desperate to have the space, both physical and emotional, to be their most creative, impassioned, calm, and authentic selves.

Particularly during COVID, women are struggling to find the time to be alone to contemplate, reflect and create.

Anne Morrow Lindbergh also wrote of this need for solitude in her seminal work, *Gift from the Sea*:

> "Every person, especially every woman, should be alone sometime during the year, some part of each week, and each day . . . Actually these are among the most important times in one's life—when one is

alone. The artist knows he must be alone to create; the writer, to work out his thoughts; the musician, to compose; the saint, to pray. But women need solitude in order to find again the true essence of themselves: that firm strand which will be the indispensable center of a whole web of human relationships. A beautiful image to hold in one's mind is to be the still axis within the revolving wheel of relationships, obligations and activities."

I found an equally compelling argument for that kind of individual space from an unlikely literary source—one of my favorite children's books!

The Story of Ferdinand by Munro Leaf is the story of a little bull who was so unusually calm and peaceful that no one could quite understand him. Rather than running and jumping and butting heads with all the other little bulls, Ferdinand chose to sit quietly and smell the flowers under his favorite cork tree.

I recall reading the book to my younger brothers and then, decades later, to my kids, marveling at how gentle and loving the bull was. I wondered what was so wonderful about sitting alone under that tree. I didn't yet know the value of that alone time. The truth is I didn't yet know how to sit quietly and smell the flowers! The instinctual need for solitude and calm didn't come easily to me.

A ROOM OF ONE'S OWN

For me, meditation has been instrumental in my journey to cultivate that appreciation for solitude and accompanying ability to be calm and centered.

In bullfighting, a bull often finds a spot (querencia) in the ring where he can pause, feel safe, and regain his strength and power. When the bull is enraged, the matador is in charge, but when he finds his querencia and calms down, he is at his most powerful.

Whether we have a room of our own or a spot in the bull ring, it is the experience of finding our calm, our place of peace, where we can connect with ourself, and regain our strength and power that is critical.

For me, there is nothing like a long walk on the beach.

It is where I get that sense of peace, that inner calm, and from where I am able to garner my strength, my resolve, my power for the day.

The Gift from the Sea is set at the seashore and, as the sea tosses up its gifts of shells, so the mind brings up its own treasures.

Lindbergh continues:

> I want first of all . . . to be at peace with myself. I want a singleness of eye, a purity of intention, a central core to my life that will enable me to carry out these obligations and activities as well as I can. I want, in fact—to borrow from the language of the saints—to live "in grace" as much of the time

as possible. I am not using this term in a strictly theological sense. By grace I mean an inner harmony, essentially spiritual, which can be translated into outward harmony. I am seeking perhaps what Socrates asked for in the prayer from the Phaedrus when he said, "May the outward and inward man be one." I would like to achieve that state of inner spiritual grace.

It is our challenge to find a place, both physical and figurative, where we can journey inward, find our calm, and garner our strength.

Joseph Campbell also spoke of the importance of having a sacred space—a place without human contact, a place where you can simply be with yourself, and be with who you are and who you might want to be.

He viewed this place as one of creative incubation, saying that even though creativity might not happen right away when you're in this special space, just having it tends to ignite the muse in each of us. He went on to say that the modern-day "sacred space" is what the plains were for hunters.

Do you have a place where you can be uninterrupted?
A space where you always feel welcome and at home?
Where you can write and reflect?
Cry?
Is it time to create one?

A ROOM OF ONE'S OWN

Having our own sacred space is vital to emotional, psychological, and spiritual well-being, but there are times when it is impossible to have one's own actual place, so we need to create space in our own minds to find that calm, that security, that freedom.

This quote, which author Steven Covey connects to the teachings of Victor Frankl, the writer and Holocaust survivor, suggests that the space between stimulus and response is that peaceful pause, the psychological version of a querencia.

"Between stimulus and response there is a space.
In that space is our power to choose our response.
In our response lies our growth and our freedom."

Pausing before talking, writing, texting, or emailing creates that inner space.

Think about a time this week when you reacted to something that you heard or read or saw without pausing.

What might have been different had you taken a breath and paused before reacting?

As a mother of four, I can think of a myriad of moments when a longer breath would have allowed me to reflect more before reacting.

A helpful reminder is to repeat the word, slowing on the inhalation and down on the exhalation. Slowing down encourages more careful and thoughtful responses! Let that be our mantra! SLOWING DOWN . . .

Focus on creating a space for yourself, whether in an open field, a tiny closet, or a bathtub.

Allow yourself to sink into silence and see what happens.

In the words of Marcus Aurelius, the Roman Emperor, AD 161: "It is in your power to withdraw yourself whenever you desire. Perfect tranquility within consists of the good ordering of the mind, the realm of your own."

It's not easy to find the time or the place for that solitude.

But you can always find it when you go inside and breathe.

My mission is to create a space for women to come together in an environment of love, support, and safety, where we can have meaningful discussions, connect within, and listen to our own and collective wisdom.

With love and light,
Nora

Between stimulus and
response there is a space.
In that space is our power
to choose our response.
In our response lies our
growth and our freedom.

Viktor Frankl

39

THRIVING RATHER THAN STRIVING

Dear All,

COVID has aged me.

The struggles, the losses, the feeling of being trapped, the depletion of energy, the repetition of days, all have conspired to age me considerably.

It doesn't matter if others don't see that I've aged.

I see it and feel it.

Mary Pipher, who wrote the best-selling book on teenage girls called *Reviving Ophelia*, wrote a book on the topic called *Women Rowing North, Navigating Life's Currents and Flourishing as We Age*.

The title got to me. I imagined all the women I know in canoes rowing north, against the current, paddling with ferocity, while laughing and waving to one another. Just the thought of being part of something bigger than my own situation calmed me down.

One of my favorite quotes about aging is by Ingrid Bergman who wrote, "Getting old is like climbing a mountain. You get a little out of breath but the view is much better."

For me, this is a poignant reminder of the gift of aging—perspective.

Mary Pipher writes: "The core concern of this life stage, with all of its perils and pleasures, is how to cultivate resilient responses to the challenges we face. Resilience is built by attention and intention. We can take responsibility for our attitudes and focus on our strengths and joys. We can go deep and face truth squarely. We can learn the skills that allow us to adapt to anything. Yes, anything."

Her advice sounds similar to what I share with my coaching clients of all ages.

Pay attention to what's happening.

Be intentional about everything—your partner, your passion, your time.

Go deep by meditating and reflecting, and face the truth squarely.

As we age, we don't need to climb the ladder of success as defined by external forces and opt instead for more internal satisfaction.

We focus on thriving rather than striving.

Isn't that what we want at any stage of life?

I am on the cusp of significant change in my life.

In fact, it seems that every conversation I have has to do with navigating change—in my work life, my parents' lives, my children's lives, my siblings' lives.

I love the fact that Mary Pipher talks about her body aging while her soul expands. That's what I am going for and you can too.

We can hold seemingly diametrically opposed truths at the same time.

Most of us are struggling with one thing while celebrating something else. We can be facing tremendous loss and great possibility.

To be happy, Pipher continues, "We cannot just settle for being a diminished version of our younger selves. We must change the ways we think and behave …let go of the past, embrace the new, cope with loss, and experience wisdom, authenticity, and bliss."

Seems like a prescription for life, not just for aging.

Pipher outlines a number of areas that we should devote ourselves to so that we ward off the negative side effects of aging. These are a few of her suggestions for thriving:

1. A commitment to growth and being curious about everyone and everything around you
2. Acceptance, surrendering to what is
3. Embracing friends and family and leaning in to how important connection is

4. Becoming comfortable being alone; distinguishing solitude from loneliness
5. Getting to know and understand ourselves better—self-awareness
6. Making intentional choices about our priorities and how to spend our time
7. Giving ourselves "small treats" every day
8. Creating community and giving of yourself to that community

My favorite chapter has to do with "creating resplendent narratives," by which the author means thinking and speaking about one's life focused on one's strength and resilience. Learning to share from a place of pride in what we have accomplished emotionally in our life, where we have shown our true colors, embraced and overcome challenges to become the extraordinary people that we are is critical.

In the words of the Native American poet, Joy Harjo, "It is memory that provides the heart with impetus, fuels the brain and propels the corn plant from seed to fruit."

Pipher reminds us that:

"We can't change our pasts, but we can still change our stories. Stories allow us to make sense of our lives, resolve our omnipresent contradictions and understand ourselves and others. They give us context for comprehending the flow of life that constantly surrounds us . . . We can remember our history of resilient responses. We can compose narratives that serve us. We can ask, 'How did that make me stronger? What did I learn from that experience? What am I proud of when I look back?'"

Creating meaning in our lives really is our only option. And that is the case no matter what stage of life you are in.

We arrive at true meaning when we know deep in our core being that change is constant.

The best parenting advice I ever got was to remember that "everything is a stage." Critical to hold onto during the toddler and teenage years!

It's the same with life.

We can learn a lot from the Buddhist tradition which teaches that everything is impermanent.

Practitioners have always understood impermanence as the cornerstone of Buddhist teachings and practice. All that exists is impermanent; nothing lasts. Therefore, nothing can be grasped or held onto. When we don't fully appreciate this simple, but profound, truth we suffer.

Thinking about aging in this context is such a relief.

We are all aging at every moment. Every stage of life, just like everything in life, is impermanent.

THRIVING RATHER THAN STRIVING

Change is the constant.

So, we are better served to stop clinging, wishing we could stay in any particular life-stage and surrender to the one truth: Everything is impermanent.

Striving is clinging.

Thriving is letting go and being present.

I have learned a great deal watching someone I love dearly struggle with a terminal illness. His commitment to the moment is inspiring.

For him, thriving has replaced striving.

Meaning has replaced the unimportant.

Connection has replaced everything.

He knows that nothing lasts forever and he lives live with a commitment, a love, a passion for whatever he is involved with in the present moment.

Whether we are young, old, vibrant or ill, we and everything around is changes. Nothing will stay the same.

It's up to us to choose to create a life of meaning, filled with purpose and connection, making every moment count.

There's something about the Six Perfections in Buddhism that speak to me. The following qualities are considered to be the way to enlightenment. At the very least, they are—for me—wise lessons to live by:

» Generosity or giving. Rejoicing in sharing.

- » Ethics. Not harming others, not stealing, not creating problems, being honest, truthful, and kind.
- » Patience. Tolerance. Forbearance. Not getting angry. Appreciating different situations and people as a wonderful opportunity to learn.
- » Effort. Being enthusiastic in our efforts as we do everything.
- » Meditation. Learning how to make the mind attentive so we gain insights.
- » Wisdom. Seeing things how they really are, not how we want them to be.

We are instructed to use our daily life to develop these practices. It's all about bringing awareness to everything we do. When we do that, we become closer to our truest selves. We can learn to dissolve the small self and become more present to the vastness of life and love.

These "perfections" align beautifully with the lessons in Women Rowing North and together offer a helpful, realistic, and inspiring path to our own contentment.

Pipher concludes her book with "all great truths are paradoxical. We are all together and alone. Life is joyous and tragic. In a state of bliss, paradoxes can be held without tension. Everything seems so connected and inevitable."

THRIVING RATHER THAN STRIVING

Let's all breathe deeply together, allowing the sensations of both joy and pain, youth and aging, fear and love, disappointment and passion to coexist.

Be open. Embrace it all.

In the words of the poet John Quinn:

> Sometimes
> A voice is sent
> To calm our deepest fears
>
> Sometimes
> A hearty laugh
> Will banish all our tears
>
> Sometimes
> Words will wing
> Our dreaming even higher
>
> And sometimes
> A mind will set
> Our imagining afire.

May you listen to that voice, engage in hearty laugher, express your dreams, and allow for wondrous imagining.

Embrace it all and live your one life with passion and presence.

With love and light,
Nora

Sometimes
A voice is sent
To calm our deepest fears

Sometimes
A hearty laugh
Will banish all our tears

Sometimes
Words will wing
Our dreaming even higher

And sometimes
A mind will set
Our imagining afire.

John Quinn

40

A FLOOD OF TEARS

Dear All,

It's been a year since I started these newsletters.

The stay-at-home order was weird and scary and people needed hope, optimism, and ways to stay connected.

We were feeling isolated and uncertain and craved anything that brought us closer.

Along with the newsletters, I began doing Sunday night Gatherings, bringing women together for meditation, sharing, writing, and reflection.

The love for the newsletters and Gatherings has been overwhelming. They have provided comfort and solace to many, and been a salve for the confusion and loss so many of us felt.

Each week I've offered words of wisdom on topics that I thought would resonate with my readers as we faced the challenges of 2020.

I wrote about fear, compassion, resilience, equanimity, disappointment, creativity, thriving, belonging, exhaustion, and more.

People have been moved and inspired, have connected with other amazing women, and have felt seen and heard.

In many of the newsletters, I shared snippets of my personal life as they related to the topic on which I was writing.

My honesty and transparency were well received.

I shared my experiences so that my readers would feel less alone.

But I never felt exposed—just slightly vulnerable.

This newsletter is different.

This moment in my life is different.

I am going to share a deeply personal tragedy in my life, unrelated to any topic of general interest. I imagine that some of you will resonate with the story or find it touching, but I am writing it in order to bring myself back to life, after being completely disconnected for the past ten days.

In writing this, I am pinching myself, forcing myself to come to terms with what happened—to face the truth.

My brother Mark was diagnosed with cancer a few years ago.

Given his youth, excellent health, and incredible attitude, we all believed he would beat it.

But life doesn't go as planned, as expected, or as hoped.

When my brother called me last week, his breathing was labored.

A FLOOD OF TEARS

All of a sudden, the unimaginable presented itself. My brother might die.

The truth was that he was dying, but "might" was as far as my mind would allow me to go.

From the sound of his breathing, I knew I had to go and see him.

Within a few hours, my daughter and I were boarding a red-eye at Los Angeles International Airport, bound for New York.

By the time we arrived at his West Side apartment, things had gotten worse.

I walked into his bedroom where his husband and our sister were standing around the bed, staring in disbelief at Mark's condition.

Reality grabbed me with a violence I had never known. Death was happening and it didn't give a damn about fairness or my readiness.

Mark heard my voice and his eyes widened, almost popping out in surprise. He knew I was there.

I sat down next to him and instinctively knew what to do—just be with him, hold his hand, tell him how much I loved him.

He was shrieking in pain much of the time and the nurse recommended that we tell him that we would be alright and that he could let go.

As a meditation coach, I have used the term often—sharing with students the wisdom of "letting go," of "surrendering."

But this was different. I didn't want him to let go.

I wanted him to stay with me.

I told him stories, made some pathetic jokes, held back tears, and sat with him until, a number of hours later, he took his last breath.

Mark and I shared a love of theater, cooking, reading, dancing, and more.

He was smart, funny, sarcastic, brave, bossy, and beautiful.

As the Producing Director of the Working Theater in New York City, he had a clear purpose—to make theater accessible to everyone and to amplify the voices and stories of minorities, women, immigrants, and working people everywhere. He focused on essential workers before we had ever heard the phrase.

He was in an awe-inspiring, committed relationship with the love of his life for twenty years, and was finally able to legally marry just a few years ago.

He loved his family and friends honestly and fiercely.

Everyone who knew him loved him for being the supportive, creative, clear, impish, sarcastic, and wonderful man he was.

Having to tell my parents that Mark died was the most difficult thing I had ever done in my life.

A FLOOD OF TEARS

How could it be that fourteen years after the death of their youngest son, they would lose another one?

How could it be that my sister and I would lose two brothers?

I spent the week in New York City, mourning my brother's death with his husband, my parents, my children, and friends.

It was brutal, painful, surreal, and poignant.

I woke up in the mornings forgetting that he had died.

I walked around New York City imagining him in all his favorite spots.

I watched my usually stoic mother wail when she learned of his death.

I heard my father, who is ninety-five and declining in cognitive abilities, ask over and over when my brother would be coming to visit.

I ached. I lamented. I got sick to my stomach.

But I survived.

We flew back to Los Angeles a few days ago, and I've tried to process the experience.

But it's not processable.

It's just hard.

Painful.

Unfair.

Horrible.

Sad.

I came home to many beautiful condolence cards, flowers, and other expressions of love and support.

It felt like they were for someone else.

I was not home.

I feel the angst Edna St. Vincent Millay writes about: "Where you used to be, there is a hole in the world, which I find myself constantly walking around in the daytime, and falling in at night. I miss you like hell."

I am allowing myself this grief.

The words of W. S. Merwin could be mine:

Your absence has gone through me
Like thread through a needle.
Everything I do is stitched with its color.

And the days go on.

I am so grateful that I finally know how to breathe, that I can find moments of peace when meditating, allowing whatever feelings I have to just be there.

I walked on the beach today, my place of healing and transformation, and saw a school of dolphins leaping in their elegant, lyrical way. I knew Mark saw them too.

There are many things about this experience that will inform the rest of my life.

I am straining to find a lesson, something to impart to you that will make a difference.

A FLOOD OF TEARS

But I have only learned this—losing someone you love is beyond heartbreaking. It is soul-crushing and feels like something from which you will never recover.

However, the world looks different when you are in the bubble of grief.

It's an improvement over the world before the loss.

The truth is, the world would be a better place if we treated one another as if we were experiencing a crushing loss.

1. We would talk less.
2. We would choose our words more carefully.
3. We would observe what's happening more closely.
4. We would eat more carbs.
5. We would hug more and for longer periods.
6. We would let a lot of bullshit go.
7. We would be more tuned into to one another's pain.
8. We would cry more freely.
9. We would focus on what's really important.
10. We would care more deeply.
11. We would be more forgiving of ourselves and others.

12. We would be less critical about stupid things.

13. We would be more deeply connected to stillness.

Perhaps we can incorporate these honest, tender ways into our lives right now, and trust that by creating more avenues for love and acceptance, we are getting closer to our truth, our worth, our deepest selves.

I will continue to grieve for as long as I need to. And while I grieve, I will grow.

During this time, I hope to figure out how one moves on from monumental loss.

I will read and reread this poem by Tagore:

Peace, my heart, let the time for the parting be sweet.
Let it not be a death but completeness. Let love melt into memory and pain into songs.
Let the flight through the sky end in the folding of the wings over the nest.
Let the last touch of your hands be gentle like the flower of the night.
Stand still, O Beautiful End, for a moment, and say your last words in silence.
I bow to you and hold up my lamp to light you on your way.

I will honor my brother by cooking more, traveling more, communing with nature more, listening to music

A FLOOD OF TEARS

and dancing more, supporting theater more and loving my friends and family more than ever.

I am more certain than ever that my purpose in life is to do two things: write authentically and with heart, and coach women to become friends with themselves, to find their own still small voice and live according to their values, with calm, clarity, and connection at the core.

I am committed to loving more deeply and being of service always.

I am here for any of you who have or are experiencing loss, pain, confusion, or overwhelm, and together we will find peace.

With love and light,
Nora

Where you used to be,
there is a hole in the world,
which I find myself constantly
walking around in the daytime,
and falling in at night.
I miss you like hell.

Edna St. Vincent Millay

41

RADICAL LOVE

Dear All,

Last week I wrote about my little brother's untimely death and its chokehold on me.

All the stages of grief, in no particular order, are finding their way in.

Each day is different.

Some days I can't focus on a thing.

Other days I wake up forgetting that he's gone.

One day I was able to laugh at something funny.

Many days I want to throw things and shout at the unfairness of it all.

But every day is spent with a massive ache in my heart that feels like an immovable boulder.

In her memoir, *The Year of Magical Thinking*, Joan Didion writes that "grief, when it comes, is nothing we expect it to be. Grief has no distance. Grief comes in waves, paroxysms, sudden apprehensions that weaken the knees and blind the eyes and obliterate the dailiness of life."

We have all suffered losses in our lives, whether the loss of someone dear to us, the loss of a job, a friendship, a dream, or even a stage of life.

This past year will always be remembered as a year of losses.

How do we move through grief and loss?

Slowly.

Without judgment.

Open to its strangeness.

Aware of its unpredictability.

Of all the quotes and poems I've read over the last few weeks, the one that had the biggest impact on me was by the artist Nick Cave, who lost his teenage son a few years ago: "The paradoxical effect of losing a loved one is that their sudden absence can become a feverish comment on *that which remains* . . . a luminous super-presence."

How do we connect to that luminous super-presence?

How do we begin to allow in the beauty of what remains after a massive loss?

Elizabeth Gilbert, after losing the love of her life, observed: "Grief is a force of energy that cannot be controlled or predicted. Grief does not obey your plans, or your wishes. Grief will do whatever it wants to you, whenever it wants to. In that regard, Grief has a lot in common with Love."

That made me pause. Grief has a lot in common with love.

RADICAL LOVE

I'm not sure I would have been able to verbally articulate that thought, but I do have a very clear sense of what is meant by it.

My heart is wide open, every sensation I have is heightened, there's a depth, a poignancy to everything I do, see, and feel. I feel alive and present. I am closer to the truth and more connected to what matters.

Maybe seeing the connection between grief and love is what allows us to begin to find the "luminous super-presence."

I am reminded of the words of Helen Schucman, who instructs us: "Your task is not to seek for love, but merely to seek and find all the barriers within yourself that you have built against it."

Not an easy task when you are grieving or experiencing loss, and hoping that others will reach out and comfort you and make the pain go away.

But of course, like everything else, it's all about our inner work.

And so, the inquiry begins: What's between me and loving?

And the examining has to happen, even in my state of grief.

Tara Brach talks about the radical love that arises from the purity of our awareness—that cuts through the delusion that we are separate.

If we want to wake up from "habitual armoring," we have to recognize and embrace those barriers to love.

First, we have to be clear that we want to live with that open awareness, that poignancy, that depth.

Go inside, ask for guidance, ask to be shown how to awaken your heart.

Then, we have to do the investigating and embracing of the barriers to openheartedness.

Those barriers can be:

1. THINKING:
   Getting lost in the veil of thought. Rather than really being there with people, we are planning our response, caught up in our ideas. We need to come back, step outside of our thoughts, anchor ourselves with the breath, and know that we are not our thoughts.

2. JUDGMENT:
   We are addicted to judging ourselves and others. We think someone is bad or wrong, inferior versus superior. This type of judging brings aversion. We need to uncover our hidden biases in order to discover radical love. Judgment keeps us from total openness and that openness is what allows us to love.

3. WANTING :
   When we approach others with our wants, we are not fully present or open to love. We focus on our wants and our needs, and miss out on what the other person has to give us. We are forcing rather than being truly open.

4. FEAR:
   When we approach others with fear, we are blocked from love. When we are focused on how others view us and care about their judgment, we are not connected to truth or honesty. Our interest in others' opinions shuts down our capacity to learn, be mindful, and be openhearted.

WHAT ARE YOUR MOST COMMON BARRIERS TO RADICAL LOVE?

WHERE IS YOUR HEART DEFENDED?

WHERE CAN YOU BECOME MORE OPEN?

Bring a moment to mind when you weren't fully there. Take a look at what happened. Were you preoccupied? Overthinking? Worried about what they thought of you? Was there judgment? Blame? Was there an agenda? Did you want something from them?

It's a bit of a paradox. When we allow ourselves to be open, we can love more easily.

When love flows, we are open.

Grief, like love, opens us.

And despite the pain, the angst, the fear associated with it, love is the only way to live, including with grief.

The opportunity we have is to be surprised by, and then engage with, the luminous super-presence that remains after our heartaches, our grief, our unmanageable losses.

Perhaps it is a deeper love, a new perspective, a commitment to seizing the day, a freedom from fear.

Whatever remains, embrace it.

For me, what has remained after my brother's death is a commitment to bring more creativity into my life— to travel more, eat more carbs, listen to music more.

And perhaps more than anything is an unshakeable love for, and commitment to, my sister. We are very different people and have not always been close, but we are now bound together so tightly and with such a powerful love that nothing can rupture the connection.

There were four of us and now there are two. We will reimagine life. We will remember our brothers always. And we will work together to keep our small, but mighty, family strong and secure, in a snug nest of love and closeness.

May we become more openhearted. May we dismantle our barriers to love.

May we find in our grief and loss a luminous super-presence and may we live in its light.

With love and light,
Nora

Grief is a force of energy that cannot be controlled or predicted. Grief does not obey your plans, or your wishes. Grief will do whatever it wants to you, whenever it wants to.
In that regard, Grief has a lot in common with Love.

Elizabeth Gilbert

42

LET THE LOVE IN

Dear All,

Everything always comes down to love.

We've talked a lot about expanding our capacity to love everyone and everything around us.

Equally important is allowing in love and support from others. This has always been challenging for me, and even more so during this period of grief.

When you are grieving a loss, sometimes you need to be alone.

Sometimes you need to be with people.

And sometimes you have no clue what you need.

The Jewish tradition of sitting shiva immediately after the death of a loved one helps the bereaved when they are in this very unsettled state.

The mourning family opens their home and invites family, friends, and community to meet them in their grief. It is a time to share memories and stories about the deceased and honor the mourners' grief process.

The tradition is about grieving openly and allowing others to see the tears, anger, sadness, and shock that may arise in the period of immediate loss of a loved one.

But we are living in a time of COVID and, therefore, my family—like thousands of others who have lost their mothers, fathers, brothers, sisters, sons, daughters, and friends—has been without the traditional offerings of love, laugher, tears, comfort, food, and companionship.

We are grieving the grieving process.

Instead, we have the internet. Our family has received hundreds of emails and posts with condolences for Mark's death. Every one sent with the best intentions.

Why then does "I'm sorry for your loss" fall flat for me?

Maybe because I am not ready to let the love and support in.

Maybe I'm a bit numb, unable to feel how genuine the love is.

Maybe because not all condolences are alike and some people just say the wrong things.

But through my meditating and writing this week, I see more clearly that my reasons are irrelevant. All that matters is that I choose to let more love in.

My son, who is about to be ordained as a rabbi, shared a teaching about the importance of letting others support you.

LET THE LOVE IN

I learned that Moses's father-in-law insists that Moses can't do everything on his own and advises him that knowing how to delegate and ask for help is absolutely critical.

Not letting others in to help is "not good," one of the few times that phrase is ever mentioned in the Hebrew Bible.

My son reminded me of the same thing.

But it's hard to know when the painful memories will swoop in and knock me over.

The words of Colette, translated by Robert Phelps, resonate with me: "It's so curious; one can resist tears and 'behave' very well in the hardest hours of grief. But then someone makes you a friendly sign behind a window, or one notices that a flower that was in bud only yesterday has suddenly blossomed, or a letter slips from a drawer. . . and everything collapses."

Anne Lamott, in her book, *Operating Instructions: A Journal of My Son's First Year*, expresses how I feel: "And I felt like my heart had been so thoroughly and irreparably broken that there could be no real joy again, that at best there might eventually be a little contentment. Everyone wanted me to get help and rejoin life, pick up the pieces and move on, and I tried to, I wanted to, but I just had to lie in the mud with my arms wrapped around myself, eyes closed, grieving, until I didn't have to anymore."

We all have to find our own way forward, not out of, but through our grief. We need to grieve until we don't have to anymore.

Each of us journeys through grief differently.

I'm inspired to hear about other people's openness to support during hard times.

Several weeks ago, a little girl in our community was hit by a car while riding her bicycle, suffered a brain trauma and tragically died. Her mother tweeted a message asking everyone to pray for her daughter. In an interview with the *New York Times*, she described how helpless she felt when her daughter was in the intensive care unit, hoping that anyone and everyone who could would lift her daughter up in prayer. The mom also asked them to lift her up in prayer as well. Thousands of strangers from around the world reached out to her and together they communicated about life, death, religion, and family. The sharing of stories of hope sustained and comforted the family in need.

And it sustained and comforted those who wanted to help as well.

One of the women who offered her support told the *New York Times* that in an internet world of toxicity, anger, and harshness, the request by the mother gave her "a way to help. She told us we could pray for her and her daughter."

She expressed that in a time when our nation is so divided, coming together to help someone in need is positive and healing for us all.

After I read this, I tried my hand at letting others in.

I posted about my brother's death on a Facebook group I am part of, made up of women over forty. Doing so was uncomfortable for me—my cynicism kicked in.

And yet, there was something strangely comforting to read the hundreds of posts, mostly from strangers, sharing their experiences, thoughts, and words of wisdom and care.

Oddly, I felt seen. Even if by strangers.

And I recognized what my sharing did for many of the women who had themselves lost a sibling. They too felt seen.

There was even one woman who opened up that she too had lost both of her brothers. We shared that particular grief.

Allowing others to be there for us is a gift for them as well as a solace for us.

I have spent my life giving to others and I know it's time for me to be more open to the gifts of support from my family and friends.

I recall a time many years ago when I was taking a commuter train in to work every day. It was cold and

BE STILL & SOAR

rainy out, and I was carrying various bags, an umbrella, and probably a cup of coffee.

I was in the midst of a painful divorce, and was exhausted from caring for four kids, working full time, and trying to keep it together.

I didn't have the tool of meditation and was fraught with anxiety.

I stepped into the crowded train, knowing that I was teetering on a precarious edge.

A gentleman was seated in the front row and an empty seat was beside him.

I plopped down in the seat—my stuff strewn all over the place. Drops of rain from my umbrella splattered on his newspaper. He was elegantly dressed and had perfectly combed white hair. He looked at me with his piercing blue eyes and asked if I wanted help with my coat. I nodded yes, as tears came streaming down my face. He gently put his hand on my shoulders and helped me take off my coat. I remember thinking that no one had ever been as thoughtful.

To this day, I think about the kindness of this man.

Of course, there have been many many people who have done loving and thoughtful things both before and after that moment, but I will forever be struck by how much it meant to be cared for in the simplest way in that moment of need.

In many ways, that moment may have been the start of my own journey to handle my anxiety, find ways to care for myself, and ultimately to nurture women and help them manage their stress and embrace life's challenges with a little self-compassion and grace.

As a single mother of four, I think obsessively about what it takes to raise children, to give them the roots to feel nurtured, loved, safe, and grounded, and the wings to discover who they are and become independent.

I have listened to Josh Groban's performance of "You Raise Me Up," with lyrics by songwriter Brendan Graham, countless times when I need to remind myself that I am doing a decent job of parenting them all.

Today, I listened to the song and heard a new message.

One for me: that I have many to thank during this and other periods in my life when there was darkness, confusion, shame, and pain.

I thank all of you who have been there for me then and now.

Graham's lyrics are poignant and haunting. "When I am down and, oh my soul, so weary . . . / You come and sit awhile with me. . . . / You raise me up, to walk on stormy seas."

Take a listen to the whole of this gorgeous song and allow yourself to feel deep appreciation both for those who have supported you in tough times, as well as for yourself and all that you have done to raise up others in their times of need.

We really all are connected.

We really do need one another.

We awaken when we finally know we are not separate from others.

In the wisdom of the poet Yung Pueblo:

a hero
is one who heals
their own wounds
and then shows others
how to do the same

May we all honor the heroes in our lives and strive to be heroes for others.

With love and light,
Nora

It's so curious; one can resist tears and 'behave' very well in the hardest hours of grief. But then someone makes you a friendly sign behind a window, or one notices that a flower that was in bud only yesterday has suddenly blossomed, or a letter slips from a drawer . . . And everything collapses.

Collette
translated by Robert Phelps

43

ARE WE READY TO SPRING FORWARD?

Dear All,

According to the calendar, spring has sprung.

We are about to celebrate COVID-style the traditional spring holidays of Passover and Easter.

The weather is a bit warmer; the days, a bit longer.

But what does it feel like to you?

Are you ready for a season of renewal?

For many of us, what we are able to do, feel or express might still be lagging behind what we desire, wish, and hope for.

I imagine most of us are itching for that newness, that fresh start, that bold beginning.

But perhaps we aren't up to it; we may still be feeling cautious, nervous, uncertain and maybe even uncomfortable.

When I hear the word spring, I usually think of my dad who loved to point out when I had a "spring" in my step.

ARE WE READY TO SPRING FORWARD?

He loved seeing me in motion, excited about what I was about to do, almost bouncing to my next activity.

There is no such spring in my step right now.

In fact, the definition of spring that most closely aligns with my state of being is this one quoted by Annie Red Bird: "A resilient device that can be pressed or pulled but returns to its former shape when released."

We have been pressed and pulled like never before these past thirteen months, but we are resilient.

I believe we will return to our former selves with new attitudes, abilities, and outlooks once we are truly released.

I love Margaret Atwood's quote: "In the spring, at the end of the day, you should smell like dirt."

We are still in the dirt, exploring who we are becoming, still somewhat hidden and definitely not in full bloom.

We are in the process of growth, being nourished by the soil, preparing to meet the sun, and come into the light.

We can be proud that we smell like dirt because we are doing what we need to do, learning to be present, no matter where we are.

We have learned many things during this time, one of which is the simple, but masterful, teaching of Buddhist nun, Pema Chodron.

She encourages us with a single word—STAY.

Whatever state of being we are in right now, STAY. Feel what there is to feel.

See what there is to see. Imagine. Grieve. Create. Wonder. Be where you are and really be present. In the dirt. In the confusion. In the grief. In the change. In the anticipation.

And then, as the proverb says, "Bloom where you are planted."

You are exactly where you should be.

We will be released from the stagnancy, the isolation, the boredom soon.

As Pablo Neruda is quoted: "You can cut all the flowers, but you can't keep spring from coming."

Celebrate whatever spring is happening in your life.

Bloom when you are ready.

For now, we are growing, being nourished by the soil, preparing to meet the sun, and come into the light.

With love and light,
Nora

Bloom where you are planted.

English Proverb

CREDITS

All works by Yung Pueblo previously published in *Inward* by Yung Pueblo, Andrews McMeel Publishing, © 2018 by Diego Perez Lacera.

"Bewilderment" from *A Year with Rumi* by Coleman Barks. Copyright © 2006 by Coleman Barks. Used by permission of HarperCollins Publishers.

Rumi, "Search the Darkness," translated by Kabir Helminski, from *Love is a Stranger*. Copyright © 1993 by Kabir Edmund Helminski. Reprinted with the permission of The Permissions Company, LLC on behalf of Shambhala Publications Inc., Boulder, CO. shambhala.com.

William Stafford, "The Way It Is" from *Ask Me: 100 Essential Poems*. Copyright © 1977, 2004 by William Stafford and the Estate of William Stafford. Reprinted with the permission of The Permissions Company, LLC on behalf of Graywolf Press, Minneapolis, Minnesota, graywolfpress.org.

"Love After Love" from SEA GRAPES by Derek Walcott. Copyright © 1976 by Derek Walcott. Reprinted by permission of Farrar, Straus and Giroux. Reprinted by permission of Farrar, Straus and Giroux. All Rights Reserved.

Excerpt(s) from WINTERING: THE POWER OF REST AND RETREAT IN DIFFICULT TIMES by Katherine May, copyright © 2020 by Katherine May. Used by permission of Riverhead, an imprint of Penguin Publishing Group, a division of Penguin Random House LLC. All rights reserved.

BE STILL & SOAR

Excerpt from Anne Morrow Lindbergh, *Gift from the Sea*, Penguin Random House LLC.

Excerpts from Mary Pipher copyright © Mary Pipher, 2019, *Women Rowing North: Navigating Life's Currents and Flourishing as We Age*, Bloomsbury Publishing PLC. Used with permission.

"Envoi" by John Quinn, copyright © 2015 by John Quinn; from WALKING IN WONDER: ETERNAL WISDOM FOR A MODERN WORLD by John O'Donohue and John Quinn, foreword by Krista Tippett. Used by permission of Convergent Books, an imprint of Random House, a division of Penguin Random House LLC. All rights reserved.

"Separation" by W. S. Merwin, from *Selected Poems* (Bloodaxe Books, 2007). Reproduced with permission of Bloodaxe Books.

"Separation" by W.S. Merwin, currently collected in THE SECOND FOUR BOOKS OF POEMS. Copyright © 1993 by W.S. Merwin, used by permission of The Wylie Agency LLC.

Great effort was made to obtain permission for the quoted works. If there is an instance where the proper party was not contacted, the publisher would be glad to be informed and to correct future editions.

ABOUT THE AUTHOR

Nora Plesent has been supporting women personally and professionally for almost forty years.

After graduating law school, she became a prosecutor in the Sex Crimes Division of the Brooklyn District Attorney's Office, bringing justice to women who had been sexually assaulted and abused. She then founded a multi-million-dollar contract legal staffing company with the goal of creating flexible work arrangements for women trying to balance family and career. Nora is also the creator of the New Girls Network, an alliance of female leaders promoting the advancement of women in the legal profession and writes, speaks, and hosts seminars on cutting edge topics for women in the law and business.

Nora received The New York Women's Agenda Rising Star Reward in 2006. In 2013, the Los Angeles Lakers and Comerica Bank honored Nora with the LA Business Women of Entrepreneurship Award. Nora was also the recipient of the Highest Leaf Award, honoring women in business in 2016.

A single mom to four children, Nora knows firsthand the challenges of trying to do it all. At a difficult time in her life, when stress threatened her well-being, Nora discovered meditation and learned to slow down, breathe, and let go of unhelpful and recurring thoughts and expectations. She became a Certified Meditation Facilitator and now guides individuals and corporate groups to become more calm, focused, and creative. Nora has the experience, background, intelligence, and wisdom to help her clients achieve outstanding results.

In addition to her individual and group coaching, Nora founded The Gathering in 2019 and brings women together for wellness retreats focused on meditation, authentic conversation, mindful exercise, and reflective writing.

www.ingramcontent.com/pod-product-compliance
Lightning Source LLC
Chambersburg PA
CBHW020332010526
44119CB00002B/35